D0845993

ANCIENT EGYPT

ANCIENT EGYPT

Jonathan Sutherland & Diane Canwell

CHARTWELL
BOOKS, INC.

Published in 2007 by
CHARTWELL BOOKS, INC.
A division of **BOOK SALES, INC.**
114 Northfield Avenue
Edison, New Jersey 08837
USA

**Copyright © 2007 Regency
House Publishing Limited**
Niall House
24–26 Boulton Road
Stevenage, Hertfordshire
SG1 4QX, UK

For all editorial enquiries, please contact
Regency House Publishing at
www.regencyhousepublishing.com

All rights reserved. No part of this book may
be reproduced in any form or by any
electronic or mechanical means, including
information, storage and retrieval systems,
without permission in writing from the
publisher.

ISBN-13: 978-0-7858-2204-2
ISBN-10: 0-7858-2204-6

Printed in China

CONTENTS

OPPOSITE: Trajan's kiosk, Temple of Philae, Aswan.

LEFT: The goddess Hathor, Hatshepsut's mortuary temple, Deir el-Bahri.

INTRODUCTION

INTRODUCTION

Ancient Egypt, as we shall see, spanned a period of over 3,000 years, a huge expanse of time that we are accustomed to see split into different periods, known as either kingdoms or dynasties. The Ancient Egyptians, of course, did not see things this way: there is a fragment of a standing block or stele, now in Palermo, Italy, on which the kings of Egypt are simply listed, one after the other.

The somewhat arbitrary system developed by Manetho, an Egyptian priest-historian of the Ptolemaic era, is the one now in general use. Manetho divided Egypt's many rulers into 30 dynasties, based not simply on bloodlines, as we would understand the word to mean; in fact, a new dynasty was introduced whenever a gap or some other interruption in the succession occurred. To complicate matters further, this division was not always based on historical fact, but partly on mythology and partly on divisions of ruling families already established in the past. Thus we find that the king that begins the 18th dynasty was the

RIGHT: A pharoah and his queen: a modern-day re-enactment of life in Ancient Egypt. Dr. Hassan Ragab's Pharaonic Village, Cairo.

OPPOSITE: The Temple at Luxor at night.

brother of the last king of the 17th dynasty. Some Egyptologists have tried to dispense with kingdoms and dynasties altogether, but the system does give a point of reference in what would otherwise be an incredibly complicated lineage.

Another thing to bear in mind is that many of the dates mentioned are only approximate. Kings, for example, may have ruled for longer or shorter periods than is generally believed, and it is notoriously difficult to be precise. Moreover, many of the rulers of Egypt began their reigns before their predecessors had even died and may, for many years, have ruled alongside them or acted as regents. It is best to consider the dates as just another part of the framework that helps us to understand the sequence of events and major occurrences. It positively assists us, however, in being able to appreciate why a building may have been constructed at a particular time.

When we look at dynasties and kingdoms, and examine the different opinions as to their accuracy, any attempt to fathom the history of Ancient Egypt would seem to be a thankless task. It is not as hopeless as it seems, however; there is a great deal of other information; above all, the secret of Egypt's ancient language has now been revealed.

We know that Ancient Egypt was a sophisticated civilization that existed in the north-eastern corner of Africa. The kingdom was concentrated around the Nile, stretching mainly from the lower to the middle reaches of the river, but during the second millennium BC, in what is often referred to as the New Kingdom, it extended into the Nile delta. In around 1450 BC the empire established its southern limits around Jebel Barkal in the south – a small mountain lying on a large bend of the Nile, 250 miles (400km) to the north of Khartoum in the Sudan, then known as Nubia. Then at various other times, Egypt broadened its sphere of influence to include the Levant (Palestine, Jordan and Lebanon), the Eastern Desert and the Red Sea coast, the Sinai Peninsula, and the Western Desert, which we now know as Libya.

In 525 BC Egypt became part of the vast Persian Empire, which extended as far as India, before it was eventually defeated in a rapid and brilliant campaign led by the Macedonian Alexander the Great in 334 BC. Alexander founded many colony cities, all named 'Alexandria', along his route of conquest, spreading the Hellenistic culture as he proceeded throughout the known world. After Alexander's death, Egypt was successively ruled by Greeks (the Ptolemies), Romans and Byzantines, before Arab invaders took control in the 7th century AD.

Egypt had been inhabited by hunter-gatherers of the Stone Age period since the tenth millennium BC, and this was the beginning of what is now known as Predynastic Egypt, which lasted until around 3100 BC. By 8000 BC climate change and overgrazing had begun to affect the population settled away from the River Nile and large numbers began to migrate towards this great source of water, food and life; it was these people who would ultimately become the founding fathers of Egypt's unique civilization.

Recent studies show that present-day Egyptians are descended from these semi-nomadic people and that they originally came from East Africa. It was at some point around 3100 BC that a unified Egyptian state came into being, at a time when the Nile valley, from the delta to the first cataract, was being ruled from Memphis. Not only was this a time when a written language was beginning to develop, it was also when large-scale constructions were starting to appear.

Perhaps the most fruitful periods in the history of Ancient Egypt were the Old, the Middle, and the New Kingdoms. These span the 3rd to the 20th dynasties (2650–1069 BC), when the pyramids and magnificent temples were built and the use of hieroglyphics was established. Above all, it was a time when art and artefacts were produced in large numbers. It is also likely that mummification, embalming and the preservation of bodies, both human and animal, began during the Old Kingdom. Pyramids, mummies, their coffins, sarcophagi and tombs, remain to this day an enduring image of Egypt, and are the objects most associated with this fascinating ancient civilization.

The pyramids themselves, particularly the Great Pyramid of Giza, were the products of an almost superhuman effort. Thousands of workmen and slaves toiled for years to level the ground, prepare the substructure and construct the pyramids, using methods not completely understood to this day.

Egypt is also remarkable for its magnificent mythology and long line of powerful warrior kings, such as Ramesses the Great, that distinguish it as a deeply religious, vibrant, yet aggressive nation.

OPPOSITE: Tuthmose III's Temple of Amun at Karnak.

PAGE 14: The Pharaoh Djoser's Step Pyramid, Saqqara.

PAGE 15: Khafre's (Chephren's) Pyramid, Giza.

INTRODUCTION

The tomb of the boy-king, Tutankhamun, and the treasures found therein, are familiar to countless millions of people around the world. Tutankhamun was not a particularly powerful or significant pharaoh of Egypt, yet the fact that his tomb lay undisturbed until comparatively recently makes it all the more remarkable. This is especially so, when so many of the tombs, including the pyramids, were plundered by grave robbers within months or weeks of having been sealed. Many contained vital pieces of archeological evidence that were lost in the process, but many more have fortunately been preserved and appear in collections, both public and private, around the world. For some time there was a trade in mummified bodies and sacred and ancient papyri, but they are now fortunately protected.

Thanks to Egypt's hot desert climate, there is much that has remained relatively intact, including some of the most imposing and magnificent buildings in existence, in terms of both beauty and of scale. So important and fascinating is the history, culture and language of the Egyptians that their study has a name of its own: Egyptology. Here we will examine many of its aspects, from the burial customs and great constructions of the Ancient Egyptians, to their gods and rulers – a complicated task that will be approached

LEFT & PAGES 18–19: The traditional felucca, or wooden sailing boat, used extensively in the eastern Mediterranean and particularly on the Nile in Egypt.

OPPOSITE: The columns of the Temple at Luxor are illuminated at night for dramatic effect.

in the most logical way. In beginning with the foundations of the Egyptian state, before the pharaohs took control of the Nile valley, we will be taking the first and most important step in understanding how the Egyptian civilization came into being.

It is important to understand how the Egyptians lived their lives, what they ate, what they made, and how they worshipped and why. Many pharaohs ruled over all or part of Egypt over a period of 3,000 years, and most, provided their rule lasted that long, made their presence felt. Most dedicated themselves to the glory of their gods, and the way they lived, prepared for the Afterlife, ruled their people and vanquished their enemies was intimately related with their attitude to the spiritual world. Some of the pharaohs ruled for decades, others were swept aside in a matter of months, due to age, illness or palace coups. Some pharaohs left more of themselves behind than others: those who ruled during the dark periods of Ancient Egyptian history are all but lost to memory, having left nothing to posterity but their names. Some of the pharaohs built vast tombs for themselves and temples to their gods, while others made little or no impact on Egypt's long, eventful history.

The system of religion is inextricably linked with the way the Egyptian civilization evolved. The Egyptians were a pragmatic yet pious people, and the

RIGHT: The alabaster canopic chest from Tutankhamun's tomb. The four heads used as stoppers are of Isis, Neith, Serqet and Nephthys. Cairo museum.

OPPOSITE: The Valley of the Kings, Luxor.

way they regarded their gods was far from static; this is demonstrated in the many variations that occur, both in the names of the gods and in the nature of their activities. There was no common agreement as to how the world began, and at least four different versions of the creation myth have been handed down.

No book on Egypt would be complete without examining the great construction projects and monuments that inspire us with such wonder today. To the Egyptians, the pyramids were important symbols – the means by which a dead pharaoh gained access to the Afterlife and returned to earth when he wished. The pharaohs, after all, were regarded as gods in their own right, and because they attracted what amounted to cult followings, temples were provided for their worship which would continue there after they had died. Such is the importance of their ancient buildings to present-day Egyptians, that whole temples were moved in the 1960s, so that they would be saved from inundation following the construction of the Aswan Dam; this is no less an achievement than it was when the temples were originally built.

The strange nature of Egyptian writing deserves a closer look. Hieroglyphs are a combination of recognizable objects and strange symbols, and they have never ceased to fascinate. The key to unlocking their secret was discovered by chance and ultimately led to their decoding; this provided us with a deeper

OPPOSITE: The Nile between Dendera and Luxor at sunset.

LEFT: A figure in relief, with hieroglyphs, Karnak.

understanding of the Ancient Egyptians, what they thought and believed, and how they worshipped and regarded their lives and experiences.

Egypt's vast mythology reveals a bewildering collection of gods, known by various names to the Egyptians at different times. It encompasses the creation of the universe and the various feuds that existed between the gods, as they juggled for power over the heavens and ascendancy over mankind.

At various times in its long history, Egypt adopted the expansionist view, when it waged war on its neighbours. Proud and decisive warrior pharaohs engaged in great battles, some of them remembered even to this day, as cataclysmic events continued to sweep through the eastern Mediterranean.

But as with all empires that have flourished before and since, the rule of the pharaohs eventually collapsed, and Egypt had to submit to the vibrant Persian civilization, which, in turn, was brutally subjugated by Alexander the Great. For some time after this, the Greeks ruled Egypt, almost in the tradition of the ancient pharaohs, until the Romans arrived. Egypt remained a province of Rome until the Roman Empire split and Egypt came under Byzantine domination, ruled from Constantinople. Then came the Arab conquest, the Ottoman Turks, and finally the British, before Egypt's independence was finally restored.

LEFT: An overview of the tombs in the Valley of the Kings, west bank, Luxor.

RIGHT: The Court of Ramesses II in the Temple of Luxor.

25

OPPOSITE: *The Sinai Peninsula at dawn.*

LEFT: The Arabian camel has been the means of transportation in Egypt for thousands of years, and it is only relatively recently that it gave way to motorized vehicles.

To compile a full history of Egypt would be a gigantic undertaking; therefore, this can only be an overview, a starting point, that may lead to a greater understanding and appreciation. The Egyptian civilization has the power to capture the imagination like no other on earth, and what has survived of that which was created thousands of years ago, is as fresh and vibrant as it was in the time of the pharaohs.

CHAPTER ONE
THE EMPIRE OF THE NILE

CHAPTER ONE
THE EMPIRE OF THE NILE

From the scattered remains of human habitation present in the Nile valley, and that date from up to 700,000 years ago, it is evident that other civilizations existed in Egypt before the pharaohs. There is a major difficulty in calculating dates, however, in that they need to be compared with other archeological sites around the world, which creates more problems and conjecture than it solves.

The first settlers in Egypt were undoubtedly nomadic hunter-gatherers, in that water, game, and land suitable for crops seem to have been conveniently to hand. At that time, the Nile valley was probably more temperate, with more rainfall than there is today; it is also likely that it was covered in grassland, not unlike the savannahs of Southern Africa. Indeed, this would have extended out into what is now the Sahara Desert, the oases at Karga and Dungul being all that survive of these huge areas of vegetation.

Egypt also served as a migration route between Africa and Europe. The oldest tools ever to have been found were discovered in the cliffs at Abu Simbel in the Lower Nile valley, and probably date from between 700,000 and 500,000 years ago. Signs of habitation have also been found near dried-up springs and lakes dating to the Achulean period, that extended from 250000 to 90000 BC. The most important finds were

discovered at Wadi Halfa, where the earliest house-like structures ever to have been found in Egypt were unearthed. These were simple oval depressions in the ground, also known as tent rings, which were lined with flat sandstone slabs, over which shelters made from animal skins or dried grasses would have been erected. These were semi-permanent settlements and the concentrations of artefacts found surrounding them suggest they may have been part of a village.

Another important area is now in the Libyan Desert, at Bir Sahara. At the time, this would have had steady, seasonal rainfall that would have attracted both animals and hunter-gatherers, who would have congregated around the permanent waterholes.

Some time around 100000 BC, the Sahara became a desert and people began to gravitate towards the Nile valley to escape the dry conditions. This is when stone tools began to appear, made using the almost universal method of using a stone to chip flakes of stone from a larger piece. This produced thin, sharp shards, which could be used for a variety of purposes, including hunting and domestic use.

From 100000 to 30000 BC is known as the Middle Paleolithic Period; sites dating from this time are scattered all over Egypt, from the Nile valley to the Red Sea coast, and can also be found in the southern

Libyan Desert. Their early inhabitants were still much closer to Neanderthal than to modern man, yet from the evidence of animal remains and artefacts left behind in the Nile valley, they were able to create remarkably effective hunting weapons, that could cope with large, grazing animals. The people of the Khormusan were also efficient hunters and fishermen, who kept wild cattle and used tools made from bone and hematite, while another group, known as the Aterian, were the inventors of the throwing spear. The two co-existed for a relatively long period of time.

Unfortunately, the next period, known as the Upper Paleolithic, stretching from 30000 to 10000 BC, yielded little in the way of artefacts, the barrenness of the Sahara having starved many of the settlements out of existence. Increasingly, the people of North Africa came to rely on the Nile, one of the most significant sites being that of Kom Ombo, on the east bank of the Nile in the south of Upper Egypt. Here, archeologists discovered what have become known as Sebilian tools – small, stubby implements made from flakes of hard, black diorite rock.

Modern settlements along the River Nile.

These were not the only types of tools produced during the period. Others, known as Silsillian (around 13000 BC), demonstrate how tiny blades were being created to use in arrows, darts and spears. They were small and fine and extremely efficient, and some were probably used for agricultural purposes, which indicates that basic farming had its beginnings around this time.

There were, of course, other groups in Egypt at this time, including the Halfan people, whose culture flourished between 18000 and 15000 BC, while another, the Fakhurian, lived between 17000 to 15000 BC, and were mostly concentrated in Upper Egypt.

By this time, distinct cultures were beginning to emerge. The Qada dominated the area from the second cataract of the Nile to Tushka during the 4,000 years preceding 9000 BC. They were certainly farmers, as some of their artefacts demonstrate, in that they were used to cut grass and grind seeds.

Something disastrous occurred around 10500 BC, which caused a return to hunting and gathering and the production of crop tools to tail off. It has since been discovered that there was severe flooding of the Nile, which destroyed the established farmland; there is also evidence that warfare was rife around this time, in that human remains have been found bearing penetrating

wounds, usually in the chest or back. These were young adults, the majority of whom died from a single, fatal blow. In fact, around 40 per cent of the people from this period, buried in the main cemetery at Jebel Shaba, died from piercing injuries, pointing to intertribal warfare and regular skirmishes and raids. It may also

OPPOSITE: The Nile has been used for transporting goods for thousands of years
.

ABOVE: The first of the six cataracts of the Nile is near Aswan, formerly in Nubia.

have been that newcomers to the region were being systematically slaughtered.

These new arrivals fit into the Epipaleolithic Period (10000–5500 BC), being true farmers and village-dwellers. Some 4,000 artefacts have been found at one site alone, including minute blades, beads made from the shells of ostrich eggs, and a variety of scrapers. The main site is at El-Kab, which was probably occupied only during the spring and summer months due to the Nile floods. Other new cultures also appeared in the region, though they made a lesser impact on the indigenous population. This is where complications arise, as there is a gap in our understanding of where

the Epipaleolithic Period ended and the Predynastic began. This is unfortunate, because agriculture was being developed and animals were being domesticated. It was also the time when existing writing systems were giving way to hieroglyphics.

The Predynastic Period (5500–3100 BC) saw the first organized and permanent settlements, the people having made the transition from hunting and gathering to agriculture. Goats, pigs, cattle and sheep had been domesticated and wheat and barley were now being grown. Stone objects had been joined by metal ones, and the tanning of animal hides, weaving, basketry and pottery were now a part of daily life.

There was now a big shift in the way people were buried, in that cemeteries were no longer located near to villages. Now the dead were buried in foetal positions, surrounded by artefacts, and always facing towards the west. Meanwhile, in the south of the Nile valley, the Badarian culture was almost exclusively agricultural, whereas the people in the north, known as

ABOVE: A view of the fertile land bordering the Nile between Luxor and Dendera.

OPPOSITE: The ruins of ancient Yebu on Elephantine island, situated in the Nile at Aswan.

the Fayoum, lived around oases and still hunted and fished for their food.

It is in this period that furniture appeared, and objects such as pottery were now painted and decorated, with bone and ivory combs, tableware, figurines and jewellery also in evidence. This is also

LEFT & ABOVE: The Temple of Isis, Philae.

PAGES 38–39: The masts of feluccas moored on the Nile.

Of paramount importance at this time was the unification of Upper and Lower Egypt. It is unclear which took the initiative, but it is believed to have been the north; the north's power collapsed, however, and southern kings adopted its system and became rulers of Egypt. Another common explanation is that the south conquered the north, then absorbed much of the north's culture into its own.

Who was the first king of Egypt is not immediately clear. A piece of black basalt, known as the Narmer

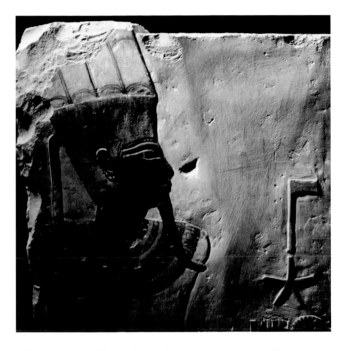

when the first hieroglyphs began to appear. These were a combination of pictograms and phonograms, a phonogram being a picture that stands not for an image but for a sound or a set of sounds connected with the image. It is believed that symbols found on some artefacts from this period, including pottery, could well have been a form of writing.

OPPOSITE: A freshwater oasis near Siwa, once famous for its Oracle of Amun.

ABOVE: A relief of Amun-Min from Deir el-Bahri, now in the Luxor museum.

RIGHT: Statue of Ramesses II wearing the double crown of Egypt, Luxor.

(Nar-Mer) Palette, is thought to depict the legendary King Menes or Meni, who had already appeared as a similar figure, but with his name in the form of a pictogram of a scorpion. It is likely that he was the first king of the unified Egypt and that the event occurred somewhere between 3150 and 3100 BC.

Egypt's first dynasty saw a united land, stretching from the Nile delta to the first cataract at Aswan – a distance of over 600 miles (1000km). The first dynasty, starting with Narmer, had eight kings, although some Egyptologists consider Narmer to be pre-first dynasty. There is also, as we have seen, a debate as to whether or not Narmer was in fact Menes, and it is not surprising that there are doubts concerning other kings of the period, and whether or not some of them may have been one and the same but counted as two.

At Abydos, in Upper Egypt, some 300 miles (480km) to the south of Cairo, there are the probable burial places of some of the earliest pharaohs. Here, a large number of artefacts have been discovered, including evidence that individuals were sacrificed during the burial of kings.

The Tablet of Menes was discovered at Naqada, on the west bank of the Nile, downstream from Luxor, the tomb in which it was found being three times larger

OPPOSITE LEFT: The temple at Semna, erected by King Tuthmose III, deifying Senusret III and dedicated to the Nubian god Dedwen. National Museum, Khartoum.

OPPOSITE RIGHT: Obelisk of Hatshepsut, Karnak.

ABOVE: An Egyptian wall painting at Deir el-Medina.

FAR RIGHT: An Osiride painted limestone pillar of Senusret I (Sesostris I), Luxor.

If we accept that Menes was the first pharaoh, then we have some confirmation in the Palermo Stone, a fragment of a fifth-dynasty basalt stele. This supposedly chronicles the first kings of Egypt, and is second in importance after the Rosetta Stone.

It is probable that Memphis was Menes's capital, and that he not only ordered a great embankment to be created to protect the city from the Nile floods, but was also responsible for the building of the Temple of Ptah. During the period of the first dynasty, Memphis was in the process of being developed and eventually would be the site of many large and important structures.

than those found at Abydos, which confuses the issue as to where the kings of the first dynasty were in fact buried. Another first-dynasty king, Aha, may have been buried at Abydos, or indeed at Naqada, but as for the others, their burial places are even more uncertain, even though references to Djer in two tombs and Den in four or five have been found.

The second dynasty consisted of nine kings, though some believe there were in fact 11, even though not all

ABOVE: Models of funerary boats in the Luxor museum, taken from the tomb of King Tutankhamun.

OPPOSITE & PAGE 46: The entrance to the Temple of Luxor, with the Court of Nectanebo and the pylon of Ramesses II.

PAGE 47: The triple barque shrine of Seti II in the Court of Ramesses II, Luxor.

of their names are known. Excavations at Umm el-Ka'ab, where royal tombs have been found, have not helped in either naming or dating some of the kings, and there is even the suggestion that kings of both Upper and Lower Egypt ruled simultaneously. It also seems to have been a period when there was war in Egypt and forays were being organized against Libyan tribes. Beyond this, nothing can be certain, neither can it be known whether or not there was a sole king of Egypt at this time.

The third dynasty lies within the period of what became known as the Old Kingdom, and probably began with a pharaoh known as Zanakht. His tomb at Saqqara was incorporated into Djoser's Step Pyramid, which is very close to modern-day Cairo. The original structure consisted of an underground burial chamber, and Zanakht may well have ruled for nearly 30 years. The third dynasty is believed to have had some nine kings, though some believe there were only six, most of them unidentifiable. Collectively, they may have reigned for anything between 75 and 214 years.

The fourth dynasty began with Sneferu, who was probably the son of Huni, the last king of the third dynasty. It is unclear how long he ruled, but it may have been for anything up to 30 years. This was a period of expansion for the Egyptians. There were campaigns against the Libyans, among others, and in Nubia alone, 7,000 slaves and 200,000 head of cattle were captured and brought back to Egypt.

The pharaohs of this period were fond of building pyramids. Sneferu was probably responsible for the northern stone pyramid at Dahshur, and may also have built two others there, including the so-called Bent Pyramid.

The second king, Khufu (Cheops), left the most significant fourth-dynasty contribution to posterity, in that he authorized the building of the Great Pyramid of Giza. He was succeeded by Djedefre, whose rule was probably short though productive. The fourth king of the fourth dynasty was Khafre (Chephren), who built his pyramid at Giza next to that of his father, Khufu. There is considerable debate as to who was responsible for the building of the Great Sphinx, which rests in a depression to the south of Khafre's pyramid. Some believe the sphinx has Khafre's face, while others believe it is attributable to Khufu.

The last builder of great pyramids on the Giza plateau was Menkaure (Mycerinus), who succeeded his father, Khafre, probably after the death of Khufu. Shepseskaf, the last king of the fourth dynasty, rapidly completed his pyramid, his tomb being in the form of a *mastaba* or 'bench', which was a forerunner of the pyramids and had a flat roof made of mud, brick or stone, with sloping sides. Because so little is known of Shepseskaf, it follows that little is known about the origins of the fifth dynasty.

Like those of the fourth dynasty, the kings of the fifth dynasty probably ruled from Elephantine, downstream from the first cataract and now part of Aswan. Temples were built during this period, first to Re (Ra) and later to Osiris, necessitating expeditions to the Sinai to find turquoise and copper; quarries were also established to the north-west of Abu Simbel to ensure a supply of gneiss, a type of granite. By now, trade with East Africa had been established and malachite and myrrh were being imported.

The last known king of the fifth dynasty was Unas: the interior of his small pyramid, situated close

to Djoser's Step Pyramid, is decorated with what has come to be known as the Pyramid Texts. The fifth dynasty came to an end after his death and his successor, Teti, married Unas's daughter, Iput, to legitimize his rule and become the first king of the sixth dynasty.

There was an unsuccessful plot to overthrow the third king of the sixth dynasty, Pepi I, and inscriptions to the effect in Egyptian tombs have allowed all the kings of the group to be identified; the sixth dynasty also comprises the last of the kings belonging to the Old Kingdom. There are believed to have been seven kings, ruling between 2345 and 2183 BC, the longest-reigning being Pepi II, who is thought to have remained on the throne for 94 years.

The last ruler of the Old Kingdom may have been Nitiqret, who not only was the first female pharaoh of Egypt, but probably also the first female ruler the world had ever seen. She was the first of only three other women to assume the title of pharaoh in her own right, the others being Hatshepsut of the 18th dynasty and Cleopatra VII of the Ptolemaic dynasty. There are some, however, who believe Nitiqret was not in fact a woman and that the mistake occurred when the name of the male king, Netjerkare Siptah I, was mistranslated.

The seventh dynasty marks the beginning of the First Intermediate Period. This encompasses the kings of the tenth dynasty, and the 11th dynasty that ruled

LEFT: Detail of the image on page 46.

OPPOSITE: Overview of the Temple of Luxor.

from Thebes. The seventh and eighth dynasties existed during a turbulent period in Egyptian history, which has led to much confusion. There have been various estimates as to the number of kings who may have ruled during this time; some believe there was no eighth dynasty at all, while others believe that the eighth dynasty was a mere duplication of the seventh. This indicates that the central authority in Egypt was breaking down; but however many dynasties there may have been, the kings were overthrown by a rival group known as the ninth dynasty.

The ninth dynasty was founded at Herakleopolis Magna, the capital of Lower Egypt during the ninth and tenth dynasties. Once Egypt had been reunified, the capital, which in old Egyptian was known as Henen-Nesut, faded into insignificance. There were probably at least four rulers of the ninth dynasty and there is considerable overlap and confusion between both this dynasty and the next.

The 11th dynasty splits into two different sections, the first being centred round Thebes. Again there is no clear indication as to how long these kings ruled or, indeed, how many kings were involved. Some Egyptologists believe there were 16 kings ruling over 43 years, while others argue there were seven over 160 years. The most important aspect of the 11th dynasty was that there was conflict among those who ruled at

LEFT: A prince and princess at the feet of Ramesses III in his mortuary temple at Medinet Habu. Their diminutive size indicates their inferior status.

OPPOSITE: The Ramesseum at Luxor.

population and administrative centre. It also has Minoan-style wall paintings that actually pre-date those found at Knossos on Crete. The probable first king of the 15th dynasty was Salitis, whose precise dates are unknown, though he possibly ruled for around 20 years. Another five kings are thought to have followed Salitis, culminating in the six-year rule of Khamudi, beginning in 1534 BC.

Almost contemporary with the Hyksos pharaohs was a group known as the 16th dynasty, which had at least 19 kings, beginning with Anat-Her and ending with Amu. Very little is known about these pharaohs, apart from their names.

The 17th dynasty was another group of Theban rulers, which ultimately opposed the Hyksos rule of Egypt and heralded in a period of unification known as the New Kingdom. There were probably ten rulers, beginning with Rahotep and ending with Kamose, who probably died around 1550 BC and took many important military initiatives against the Hyksos. In the third year of his rule, Kamose sailed north from Thebes to attack the Hyksos, marching his troops to Avaris. The whole region was laid to waste, but he nevertheless failed to take the city.

This led on to the 18th dynasty, which together with the 19th and 20th form the New Kingdom. This was undoubtedly the period of Egypt's most famous rulers, and includes the boy-king Tutankhamun. The dynasty was actually created by Ahmose, who was Kamose's brother; after the death of his brother, Ahmose picked up where Kamose had left off and drove the Hyksos out of Egypt, thereby ensuring that the 18th dynasty would rule the whole of Egypt until 1292 BC.

ABOVE: The Temple at Luxor.

RIGHT: View of the temple site at Dendera.

56

CHAPTER TWO
LIFE IN ANCIENT EGYPT

CHAPTER TWO
LIFE IN ANCIENT EGYPT

The Nile dominated the lives of the Ancient Egyptians, and tending the fertile land that bordered the river was regarded as an almost sacred duty. Annual flooding created rich alluvial soils, that supported several harvests a year, while the Nile provided water for irrigation canals. Most of the people lived in mud-brick houses they had built themselves, lived on food they grew themselves, and traded what was left for the goods they could not produce. Vegetable gardens, because they had to be located beyond the reach of the Nile's flood, had to be watered, and buckets counter-balanced on poles (*shadoofs*) were used for the purpose. Because this method of irrigation had to be operated manually, it was extremely hard work.

The vast majority of the people lived simple lives, working as farmers or field hands. The likes of craftsmen or scribes, however, belonged to a higher order in society, with the priesthood and the nobility at the very top.

Houses tended to be rectangular, usually up to around 48sq ft (4.5m²) in size. Permanent buildings did exist, made of stone, but in the main, mud for bricks would have been dredged from the Nile, straw or dried grasses would possibly have been added as a binding medium, the mixture would then be poured into

moulds, and the bricks laid out in the hot sun to dry. The dwellings built from these bricks did not last very long and when they crumbled were simply replaced, the new house built on top of the old, creating a mound or tell. After the house had been built, it was covered in plaster, similar to the adobe houses of the American South-West, and the walls were decorated, possibly

ABOVE: Farming on the banks of the Nile between Luxor and Dendera.

OPPOSITE: A demonstration of traditional Egyptian brick-making at Dr. Ragab's Pharaonic Village, Cairo.

with scenes from nature. Small windows admitted only a little sunlight, therefore the interiors were cool.

Larger houses were arranged around an inner courtyard. There would be a door in the wall facing the street, with windows on the upper floors, possibly shaded by shutters or woven mats. Doorways were usually made of stone, the doors themselves being wood, with bars on the inside to secure the house from intruders.

A typical house would have had two to four rooms on the ground floor, with an enclosed yard that doubled as a kitchen, and one or two cellars. There would be niches in the walls for religious objects and additional living space and storage could be accessed by an outside staircase.

Buildings in the towns often had two or three storeys. Many of the ground floors housed businesses and the upper floors were given over to living space, with much of the cooking done on the roof. Larger houses could have reception rooms and private quarters for visitors, while some even had lavatories, invariably with limestone seats. Sewage was simply disposed of in pits, directly onto the streets, or thrown into the watercourses. Most of the houses had floors of packed earth, but grander houses would have had floors paved with stone.

LEFT: Irrigation of the land along the Nile.

OPPOSITE: The green and fertile land bordering the River Nile.

Some copper drainpipes have been found in public buildings, such as temples, but usually water was drawn from a private or public well, which was invariably left uncovered. A spiral staircase led down to the water and the hole was usually around 16ft (5m) in diameter. The water was often polluted, or at the very least stagnant, which led to stomach and bowel complaints, which were common, and malaria, cholera, measles, tuberculosis and a host of other diseases and infections were endemic.

Heating was a rudimentary affair, being largely unnecessary, and all that was usually provided was a fire for cooking.

Small models of Egyptian gardens have been found that suggest they were rather formal, with trees or vines planted in rows, shrubs and trees for shade and fruit, and with rectangular ponds. The Egyptians also liked flowers, such as daisies, roses and jasmine.

An entire village, built during the New Kingdom, was discovered close to the Valley of the Kings at Deir el-Medina, its dimensions being some 164 x 427ft (50 x 130m), enclosed by a wall. Most of the houses were built of stone, possibly because the site was too

ABOVE: Temple of Seti I, Abydos.

OPPOSITE: A temple screen depicting Amenhotep and Hathor, Deir el-Medina, Luxor.

far from the Nile for mud brick to be used. The main
street is around 6–10ft (2–3m) wide and the average
house measures 13 x 66ft (4 x 20m); it is unlikely that
any of them were much more than single-storey
dwellings. The people who lived in them, with their
families, were the craftsmen, masons, sculptors,
painters and scribes working on the royal tombs. But
compared with these relatively modest homes, which
after all were little more than temporary
accommodation, another building, known as the
House of Djehutinefer, indicates an altogether
different way of life. Djehutinefer was a treasurer and
royal scribe during the reign of Amenhotep II. He
lived and died in Thebes, which is where drawings of
his rather more magnificent townhouse were
discovered. The house was probably three-storeys-
high, with rooms so large and lofty, averaging 23 x
33ft (7 x 10m), that supporting pillars had to be
installed. The family would have used the two top
floors and the servants the ground floor; like many
such households, the house was also used as business
premises, with weaving and spinning possibly being
the main occupation.

At best, town planning was haphazard. There
were many reasons why new settlements needed to be
established and the way in which a town was laid out
depended mainly on its location, its proximity to
water, and what local building materials were
available. With little or nothing in the way of
foundations, buildings were always collapsing; while
mud-brick buildings would simply collapse if they
became too damp, stone buildings would invariably
simply subside. New buildings were usually erected
over the debris of collapsed structures.

However, there are some cases where town planning seems to have been effective. A good example of this is Hotep Senusret – a town inhabited for around 100 years and founded by Senusret II. The city was surrounded by a brick wall before being divided into two parts by a second. Inside were large houses, with up to 60 rooms, while hundreds more had only one or two. The main street was 30ft (9m) wide, but some of the alleyways and streets in the poorer section of the city were only 5ft (1.5m) wide. Running alongside the streets were stone channels that were used as drainage.

Another city that seems to have been planned with some competence was Akhetaten, where there were open public spaces planted with trees. There were large government buildings, while workers lived in crowded flats; significantly, the workers' part of the city was walled in, while the rest of the city was not.

Temple districts in most cities were well-planned, the individual temples built in symmetrical forms and surrounded by walls. In order that sacred processions could take place unimpeded, it was vital that roads led directly through the city to the temple. In fact, the paved streets near the Great Pyramids are some 16ft (5m) wide. Although temples were originally set in open spaces, over time, residential housing would have begun to encroach, and with buildings collapsing at intervals all around, temples would eventually have had

LEFT: A view of the temple at Luxor.

RIGHT: Family statue of a husband and wife.

the appearance of lying in depressions, with the city piling ever higher up around them.

Royal palaces were, of course, most important: it was necessary for them to be large, not only because

the pharaoh's immediate family needed to be accommodated, but also because the sundry collection of second wives, concubines and their children, together with the dozens of servants, all needed to be housed. Palaces were usually enclosed and situated close to temples and administrative buildings, while craftsmen were constantly on hand to make running repairs and build extensions when required.

Towns and cities in Ancient Egypt were not the safest of places. Setting aside the perils of war or invasion, roving Bedouin tribes were always on the lookout for opportunities to plunder rich settlements, and it was often necessary for the buildings, and the towns in which they were situated, to became strongholds in their own right. As we have seen, private dwellings tended to have few points of access at ground level, but palaces needed more stringent protection. They would be surrounded by walls and gatehouses, and there would be the inevitable garrison of troops, poised to repel intruders.

The same could be said of temples, since they were often the repositories of artefacts of great value as well as being sacred objects. They, too, were walled, with tower-like structures, known as pylons, guarding their entrances; these were not only practical, in terms of defence, but also symbolic.

From various artefacts and wall paintings we know a great deal about the clothes the Ancient Egyptians wore. These were predominantly light, due to the climate, and invariably made of linen; it was only during the Roman period that cotton was used. Small amounts of silk were available and priests and pharaohs, in particular, wore animal skins, with pharaohs also sporting feathers and sequins.

Many people were involved in the production of linen, when the flax plant was turned into fibres; these would then be spun into thread and woven on horizontal looms before being made into clothing. Linen for garments was usually left in its natural state, the colour ranging from off-white to pearl-grey, though coloured garments could be purchased by the wealthy. Fabric was dyed by smearing ochre or plant extracts onto the cloth, or the yarns could be coloured before they were woven. Fine linen was often bleached by rubbing it with natron or sulphur, before spreading it on a stone slab, beating it with a club, rinsing it, and then allowing it to dry in the sun. White linen was very special in that it inferred holiness and purity. Basic colours available to the Ancient Egyptians were blue, red and yellow, and other colours could be created by using a mixture of two or more dyes. A purple colour was achieved by weaving red and blue threads together.

Clothes were relatively simple. Men wore a garment resembling a kilt or short loincloth, while slim dresses with shoulder straps were preferred by women. The

LEFT: Demonstrating how cloth was woven in Ancient Egypt.

OPPOSITE LEFT: A man of the 18th dynasty, wearing the gold of honour bestowed on the elite. Luxor museum.

OPPOSITE RIGHT: Relief from the Temple of Seti I, Abydos.

PAGES 74–75: The bountiful Nile still supports both farming and fishing, as it did in the time of the pharaohs.

length of the kilt changed over time: during the Old Kingdom it was short, but by the Middle Kingdom it reached the calf. Sometimes the cloth was pleated, then simply wrapped around the hips and held at the waist by a belt, with little or no sewing involved.

A robe, known as the *kalasiris*, was also worn, covering either one or both shoulders, that reached down to the ankles and up as far as either the breastbone or the neck. Some of the robes were sleeveless and could be worn tight or loose according to taste. A belt was used to hold the folds of the robe together; in effect, the robe was a simple rectangle of woven or knitted fabric, larger than the finished

article, with a hole in the centre for the head. The rectangle was then folded in half and the lower parts of the sides stitched together, leaving openings for the arms.

Women's dresses were sometimes pleated or adorned with beads, and depending on the period, either covered the breasts or left them bare. Capes were also worn, as were shawls.

Slaves, and people engaged in physical labour, wore cut-down versions of either the loincloth or the *kalasiris*. Egyptians were not in the habit of wearing headdresses, though some wore wigs, which could be particularly elaborate during the New Kingdom

period. It is unknown whether pharaohs wore their crowns every day or simply on ceremonial occasions.

Clothes were washed using a mixture of castor oil and saltpetre, and while the poor ran the risk of attack from crocodiles by using the river to wash their clothes, the better-off would have had their clothes washed for them.

Egyptians usually went barefoot, though occasionally they would wear sandals, which were secured by two thongs and often had a pointed tip that turned upwards. They were made either of leather or rushes, were stitched, and invariably had leather soles and straps. The wealthier wore more elaborate sandals and even ones that were made of gold. Indeed, 93 sandals were found in Tutankhamun's tomb, some of which were made of wood; others were more elaborate, but most were of normal construction. As time passed, footwear became a symbol of wealth and power and during the New Kingdom some Egyptians, directly influenced by Hittite designs, even wore shoes.

Jewellery and ornaments were not only seen as adornment. To the Ancient Egyptians they also reflected social status, religious affiliations and personal wealth. They were also used to make an individual more attractive, both to other people and to the gods. But jewellery also had a practical purpose, in that it represented an individual's savings and could be

OPPOSITE: A wall painting from the private tomb of Menna, Tombs of the Nobles, west bank, Luxor.

RIGHT: Threshing corn, another re-enactment of life in Ancient Egypt.

rings were also worn, both as decorative items and as seals, used as stamps of authority, many of which were made of bronze, gold or even slate.

Necklaces or collars were frequently worn. The *wesekh* was a broad, gold collar, worn by the pharaohs of the 18th dynasty; later it was worn either by priests or priestesses, or by dignitaries who had served the state well. Pectorals, decorated with religious scenes, which were effectively amulets, were often to be seen, while amulets were also worn as pendants around the neck; these were often given to small children to ward off evil spirits, blamed for the high infant mortality.

The Egyptians liked to paint their bodies, and women, as well as men from the upper classes, applied red ochre to their cheeks and lips and blackened the area around their eyes. Tattooing was also popular: slaves, for example, were given practical tattoos on their hands, bearing the names of their owners. Otherwise, dots, lines and geometrical shapes were de rigueur, the pigment being of a blue-black colour inserted under the skin by means of fishbone needles. It seems the Egyptians had acquired this practice from the Nubians, who created designs on the thighs of their dancing girls and musicians. The Egyptians, however, believed that tattooing had a bearing on sexuality and fertility.

In addition to water, the Egyptians also drank beer, wine and milk. As far as water was concerned, while

sold, should the need arise. A man would often discard his jewellery when he was defeated in battle.

Initially, ornaments would have been made from stones, clay, bone, ivory, resin and shells, but metals such as silver, gold, bronze and copper were eventually used. Some of these materials were disproportionately expensive, either because they were difficult to obtain or had to be imported from a distant land. Bracelets

were popular, made predominantly from bone, ivory or gold, while buttons, which performed no useful function, apart from decoration, were sewn onto clothes, and during the Middle Kingdom were most often made of bone. The Egyptians, unlike the Nubians, for example, who favoured nose and lip studs, preferred earrings and ear studs, and were particularly popular during the early New Kingdom period. Finger

ABOVE LEFT & OPPOSITE: Farming methods in modern Egypt are much the same as they were in ancient times.

there may have been sufficient, the quality was not particularly good. The people had learned from bitter experience that Nile water was unsafe to drink, so they resorted to well-water, which was not much better.

The Egyptians also brewed beer, believing it to have been the gift of the god Osiris. The same method is used in Sudan today, where a quantity of grain is coarsely ground and a quarter of it soaked and left in the sun. The rest is used to make well-leavened loaves of bread, which are lightly baked. The loaves are then crumbled and mixed with the soaked grain, which by this stage has begun to ferment. Water is then added to the mix, which

is left to ferment again. Once fermentation is complete, the liquid is strained and ready to drink. In hot countries, however, the beer did not keep for very long, and was made as required. Large-scale production in Ancient Egypt was regarded as a royal industry, and some temples had their own breweries. While bread, olive oil and vegetables made up most of the wages received by working men, a ration of around 7 pints (4 litres) was the standard beer allowance each day.

The Egyptians, of course, kept animals, including goats, sheep and cattle, and their milk was placed in egg-shaped earthenware jars. If it was not to be drunk soon

after milking, it would be made into a substance resembling yoghurt. The Egyptians also made butter, cream and cheeses and their butter is thought to have been used in a liquid state, rather like the Indian ghee.

Red and white wines were commonplace by the 18th dynasty. Each temple had its own vineyard, which produced wine used mainly in religious rituals. Otherwise, wine tended to be a rich man's drink and some pharaohs had official wine-tasters of their own.

The grapes were collected and placed in a low, wide vat, made of stone. They would then be trodden down and the juice extracted. The grape skins were then put

Egyptians tended to drink wine from shallow bowls or from vessels with short stems. For a time it was the practice to add seawater to the wine, in the belief that it improved the taste. Other alcoholic beverages, including palm wine, or alcohol derived from carob trees or poppy seeds, were also drunk, usually brewed at home.

The staple diet of the Ancient Egyptians was bread and beer, supplemented by onions, various other vegetables, and dried fish. Many Egyptians did not eat any other meat apart from fish. The rich, however, ate almost anything, including waterfowl and a wider variety of vegetables.

In the case of ordinary people, the kitchen was often located either on the flat roof of the house or in a corner of the courtyard. Cooking tended to be done in clay ovens, fuelled by wood or occasionally charcoal. Salt was occasionally used, and oil, garlic, onions and radishes were added for flavour. Local herbs and spices

FAR LEFT: Relief from the Temple of Seti I at Abydos.

ABOVE: A procession in the Anubis chapel of Hatshepsut's Deir al-Bahri temple, Luxor.

OPPOSITE: Wheatfields viewed from the Ramesseum,

into sacks and given a further pressing. Fermentation took place in open jars, sealed with a plug, before being marked with the date and location of the vineyard. To prevent the wine from turning sour, it was either poured into new jars or boiled.

included mustard seeds, cinnamon, rosemary, coriander (cilantro), vinegar and cumin. The Ancient Egyptians probably marinated their meat and fish in beer, or possibly added honey, grape juice or dried fruit to make it tastier.

While sieves, ladles and whisks were used to prepare food, the Egyptians ate with their fingers, with a small bowl of water set alongside to wash their hands. Whereas the rich ate from tableware made of gold, silver or bronze, commoners made do with clay.

Bread was extremely important, being a source of food for both animals and human beings. Grinding cereals was looked upon as women's work and only

sufficient barley, wheat or millet would be ground for immediate use. However, the abrasive action involved in the grinding process meant that tiny particles of sand and stone were left behind in the flour. Bread was simply flour and water, mixed with either sourdough or leaven. By the time of the New Kingdom, larger ovens had begun to appear, allowing several loaves of bread to be baked at the same time.

Where the ordinary people were concerned, meat was reserved for special occasions. All kinds of waterfowl, cranes, quails and pigeons were consumed, and a variety of domesticated animals were reared, including geese; until the New Kingdom period,

antelopes were also kept and eaten. Pork consumption was rare and anyone connected with the animal was regarded as an outcast and shunned.

As already mentioned, dried fish was an important part of the diet. Richer Egyptians tended to avoid fish, regarding it as unclean, though perch, eels, mullet, carp and catfish were commonly consumed. After the fish had been caught, it was cleaned, cut up, then either boiled, roasted, pickled or dried.

Cattle were often killed in temple slaughter yards, particularly because they would have been offered to the temple during their lifetime. As part of the ritual, a rope was attached to the nose ring and the lower lip, then tied to one of the animal's legs and passed over the back. It was then wrestled to the ground, its throat cut, and the blood was collected. The animal was then skinned and butchered and its remains cast into the River Nile.

Egyptians usually had their own gardens, where fruit and vegetables were grown all-year-round, due to the equable climate and fertile soil. These included radishes, celery, lentils, melons, cucumbers, endives, cabbages and coriander, while leeks, onions and garlic were also widely grown; the poor ate the roots of the papyrus plant. Lettuce leaves were eaten whole, having been dipped into oil and salt, and were thought to be aphrodisiacs. Fruits such as dates, apples, plums,

ABOVE LEFT: A papyrus showing images of gymnasts.

OPPOSITE: Pottery-making in the ancient style at the Pharaonic Village, Cairo.

pomegranates, pears, almonds, cherries, figs, grapes and peaches were grown, and imported coconuts were popular. Some of the fruits, such as grapes, figs and dates, were dried, so that they could be eaten later.

Olive trees had never thrived in Egypt, so most olive oil had to be imported, with the result that vegetable and nut oils were more commonly used. Oils were also obtained from linseed, sesame seeds and almonds.

When ordinary Egyptians were not working, they liked to sit around a lamp or fire at home, drinking beer, eating sweetmeats, and telling stories or singing songs. The rich, however, preferred rich banquets: men and women always sat apart, the host in a chair and the guests on floor mats, low stools or cushions. Storytelling, music and dancing were popular entertainments, as were wrestling matches.

While alcoholic drinks was popular, and probably safer than drinking milk or water, some Egyptians were not averse to taking mind-altering drugs. The blue lotus flower was believed to be psychoactive, hashish was used, and the effects of opium, mandrake, nicotine and cocaine had certainly not escaped their notice.

In Egyptian society, men had more social and sexual freedom than women, but sexual misconduct, which included homosexuality, ranked high in the list of serious crimes and could bring ruination or death to the perpetrator.

Both adults and children enjoyed games. Group wrestling was popular and in the event of rules being broken, offenders would be kicked and punched or even flogged with sticks. Tug-of-war, acrobatics, jumping, running, and even ball games were also popular; black-and-white marbles have been found that

LEFT: Queen Hatshepsut's mortuary temple, Deir el-Bahri.

ABOVE: A stone mason in the process of making repairs to the temple.

Though it certainly had its share of turbulent times, Ancient Egypt was still a relatively peaceful country. The vast majority of Egyptians tended to stay within their own social groups, the better-off enjoying the rights and privileges won for them by their ancestors. Usually they had inherited property, status and position, but it was occasionally possible for an enterprising person, possibly one who had made a lot of money, to better himself. Servants, for example, could inherit their master's possessions in the absence of legitimate heirs, which was another chance to advance socially. But on the whole, those fortunate to have found a niche in civil administration or the military, usually stayed put, knowing they could rely on a stable existence and a good standard of living.

There were two other powerful and distinctive social groups, the first being the military, the second the priestly caste. From time to time, both were closely linked; officers were often part of the royal administration and at the same time priests, the pharaoh being the high priest who could appoint his close friends and relations to important positions. After some time, however, the priesthood became hereditary, when its power greatly increased.

Noblemen tended to lead Egyptian armies into battle, but mercenaries came to be used more often as time passed. During the Middle Kingdom, Nubia provided many soldiers, while the Sherden and Sea Peoples were used during the New Kingdom, with Ionians, Jews and Greeks later on. Peasants, however, usually made up the bulk of the infantry, and were conscripted as required.

Before the New Kingdom, Egyptian armies were relatively small, and young men were enlisted from the

Hardly considered members of society at all, was the group of individuals known as the outcasts. These were the beggars, outlaws, social misfits and, surprisingly, those whose job it was to carry out mummifications.

towns and villages. It is difficult to guess the length of service required, especially if conscripts were used in wars of expansion rather than in home defence, or to suppress local rebellions. Eventually, these conscripts were replaced by full-time armies or forces primarily consisting of foreign mercenaries.

Egyptians were expected to pay taxes and customs duties, and to comply when required to provide labour for the pharaohs' major projects. There were various complicated ways of assessing tax, and in the case of farmers, size of fields, crop yield, numbers of animals and other methods were used. It was difficult to supervise the activities of every individual, and when foreign powers took control of Egypt's civil administration, they invariably kept the existing tax system in place. Tax collectors were widely used and accountable to district governors. They were required to issue tax receipts and account for every penny they had collected. It seems that around ten per cent of the value of imported goods was levied as customs duties, and everything that came into the country was listed to prevent, or at least suppress, smuggling.

OPPOSITE & PAGES 90–91: Ruins of the Yebu Temple of Satis, Elephantine Island, Aswan.

LEFT: The Qattara Depression: this lies within the triangle formed by El-Alamein, Mersa Matruh and the Siwa Oasis.

Chapter Three
THE EARLY PHARAOHS

CHAPTER THREE
THE EARLY PHARAOHS

Central to Egyptian society and religion was the idea of kingship and the status of the pharaoh, who was considered to be both mortal and divine. Ideally, it was the ruling monarch who selected an heir to inherit the crown; this ensured there would be no mistake regarding his right to rule and therefore his divinity. It also helped to avoid power struggles rom occurring after a pharaoh's death.

There has been some conjecture as to the origin of the word pharaoh. *Per-aa* literally means 'great house', and when translated into Greek becomes 'pharaoh', which over a period of time came to be applied to the king himself. More precisely, the term *per-aa* was used to describe the state or the royal court, in the sense that it was responsible for controlling and taxing lesser houses, known as *perw*.

The first kings of Egypt would later become Egypt's most famous gods. It is difficult to know whether or not some of these individuals actually existed, and we do not know the parts of Egypt they may have ruled. It only becomes possible to recognize specific kings towards the end of the Predynastic Period – the time prior to Egypt's unification. The first pharaoh of Egypt is thought to have been Narmer, Menes or Aha. These may have been three different entities, however, ruling in succession, or they may have

been a single person known as Narmer, with Menes and Aha his alternative names.

It is from this pharaoh or pharaohs, therefore, that the Egyptian line stretched, in one form or another, over 3,000 years, effectively ending with Cleopatra VII. There are over 170 pharaohs that can be actually named, and it is accepted that the vast majority were male, though even female monarchs in their own right were also referred to as pharaohs. The pharaoh, whether male or female, was an absolute, all-powerful monarch and the central pivot of Egyptian society and religion. It was in the pharaoh's name and through his or her power that the bureaucracy controlled Egypt.

Next in order of importance, at least for a long period in Egyptian history, was the vizier – in effect a chief counsellor, prime minister or chancellor – responsible for guiding and instructing the various levels of the bureaucracy.

Many of the pharaohs were regarded as incarnations of Horus, the falcon god, the son of

LEFT: A depiction of the god Horus in the Temple of Isis, Philae.

OPPOSITE: Columns and colossi at the Temple of Luxor.

Osiris, who had been slain by his brother Set. Therefore, the burial of a predecessor was a vital part of the accession process, requiring the correct procedure that re-enacted the last rites that were administered by Horus to Osiris. In some cases, this meant that the individual who organized and performed the ritual was not of the direct bloodline of the deceased pharaoh; it was the performance of the ceremony itself, however, that made the ritual legitimate. More often than not, however, succession fell to the elder son, in which case the father would allow his son to be co-regent. There were practical reasons for this: firstly to ensure direct succession without challenge, and secondly to ease the heir's passage towards his role of pharaoh. This practice has made it confusing for historians of Ancient Egypt, in that some sons may have borne the same name as their fathers, or the son was effectively already the pharaoh in all but name, having ruled before he officially came to the throne.

In effect, the pharaoh was a god-king – the high priest of each and every god in the Egyptian pantheon, and offerings made to the gods by his subjects were made in his name. As the supreme warlord, the pharaoh more often than not led his troops into battle. His right to rule could not be challenged because he was divine; it was believed that a god, having assumed the form of the father of the new pharaoh, created a new divine ruler when he impregnated his wife.

OPPOSITE: The Philae temple, Aswan.

RIGHT: Standing statues at Karnak.

Old Kingdom period, the entire Egyptian state was also brought to a virtual state of collapse.

Most of the evidence regarding the names and dates of each of the pharaohs comes from lists made during the New Kingdom period, some of which have been authenticated by archeological finds; but there are some parts of Egyptian history, referred to as the Intermediate Periods, where our knowledge of Egypt and its rulers is scanty to say the least.

Manetho, an Egyptian priest-historian, divided the Egyptian pharaohs into 30 dynasties, though it has since been discovered that some of these divisions are rather arbitrary. Sometimes the rule of royal families spanned dynasties, while others ruled simultaneously in other parts of Egypt. This is complicated even further by the fact that some historians believe that, here and there, Manetho got the pharaonic sequence wrong.

While we do not know precisely what the pharaohs looked like, we do know from various artefacts what they wore and how they used the royal regalia as symbols of their power. From the Early Dynastic Period, pharaohs had been wearing the double crown, signifying their rulership over both Upper and Lower Egypt. Coupled with a sceptre or staff, the crowns

FAR LEFT: Sculpted head of a pharaoh of the Old Kingdom. Luxor museum.

LEFT: Osiris, Lord of the Underworld. West bank, Luxor.

OPPOSITE: Statue of the falcon god Horus at the Temple of Edfu.

The king had major responsibilities, and his actions were seen as having a direct effect on the Nile flood. If he behaved correctly, kept order, and allowed himself to be guided by the gods, then the Nile would provide a good harvest. But in the event of catastrophe befalling Egypt, it was the pharaoh himself who was to blame; in some cases, as would be the case at the end of the

signified the pharaoh's authority and also served as charms or protective amulets.

There were many different types of sceptre; some were copper rods, with thick, golden bands, while others were of wood, carved to resemble reeds. The *heqa* sceptre was rather like a crook, in effect a cane with a hooked handle, and was sometimes given copper bands or was gold-plated. The crook symbolized the power of the king and mention of it in hieroglyphs signifies 'rule' or 'ruler'. Another type was the *was*, a straight staff, usually with a dog-headed handle and finished with two prongs. This is taken to mean dominion over both heaven and earth.

An enduring feature present in many representations of pharaohs, including that of Tutankhamun, is the rearing cobra, positioned at the king's forehead. This object, known as the *uraeus* or 'eye of Re', is taken to be a talisman or amulet, protecting the pharaoh from his enemies.

A number of different crowns were worn: the red crown, also known as *deshret*, probably originated in Upper Egypt, as did the white crown or *hedjet*, while the double crown or *pschent* signifies the rule of both Upper and Lower Egypt. The king would not only have worn the double crown: many of the pharaohs are also depicted wearing the white crown, while other variations include the *atef* crown, which was effectively a white crown with a plume on either side and with a disk on the top. The blue crown, as worn by Ramesses II (Ramesses the Great), is closely associated with war, and was probably made of cloth decorated with golden disks, while the sphinx wears the *nemes* headdress, which, from time to time, pharaohs were also in the habit of wearing.

OPPOSITE: *Temple of Qertassi with Hathor-headed columns, Kalabsha, Aswan.*

ABOVE: *King Menkaure, flanked by the goddesses Hathor and Isis. Cairo museum.*

RIGHT: *Restoration in process on the site of the Djoser Step Pyramid at Saqqara.*

According to legend, not only was Menes the first king of the first dynasty, he was also responsible for creating a unified Egypt. He probably ruled for around 60 years and among his other achievements was the founding of the city of Memphis. Menes also established many of the cults in Egypt, formulated Egypt's first laws and, according to some, even invented writing. There has always been considerable debate regarding these early kings, but in terms of their impact on Egypt at large, Menes was probably the greatest of his line. He ruled during a period of expansion, when the Egyptians were extending their influence to the first cataract of the Nile, and raids were being organized against the Nubians. He had a

strong capital in Memphis, that was easy to defend, located as it was on an island in the Nile. His chief wife was Queen Berenib, but she was not the mother of Djer, his heir. Legend tells that Menes, otherwise Narmer or Aha, met his death when he was attacked by wild dogs and crocodiles at the Fayoum Oasis.

Menes's son, Djer, ruled for 57 years and also led campaigns into Nubia. Excavating at Saqqara, archeologists have discovered wooden tablets, which hint at a practice that was then dying out in Egypt, that of human sacrifice. However, Djer's large tomb at Abydos contains the remains of 300 retainers, probably ritually sacrificed, so that they could accompany the king when he was buried.

We do not know for certain if the next king, Djet, was in fact the son of Djer, but he may have reigned for 23 years. Again, upwards of 170 retainers were put to death when the pharaoh died, their purpose being to serve him in the Afterlife. This was also a practice that would eventually die out, because later kings began to substitute symbolic workers or servants (*shabtis*), to accompany them and serve them in their tombs.

When Den came to power he was probably quite young, but he lost no time in limiting the power of Egyptian officials, who had grown too influential during the rule of his predecessors. Thereafter, all power was concentrated on the pharaoh. It is known that Den organized campaigns into Palestine and after successful conclusions, brought back a harem of female prisoners. He also ventured into the Sinai Desert to track down Bedouin raiders. Den's tomb at Abydos is unique in that it is the first example in which granite was used, its huge red-and-black slabs, brought from Aswan, having been used to create the floor of the burial chamber. Also of interest is the stairway, which has a sealed wooden door, guarded by a portcullis to prevent grave robbers from entering.

Den may well have been the father of the next pharaoh, Anedjib, whose name means 'safe is his heart', and who is believed to have ruled for around 26 years. During his rule there were revolts in Egypt and it is possible that Semerkhet, whose name means

OPPOSITE: Herders in the Nubian desert.

ABOVE LEFT: King Seti I making an offering to the goddess Hathor, Temple of Seti, Abydos.

'thoughtful friend', defeated Anedjib, which is possibly why Semerkhet was omitted from the Saqqara king list.

The last king of the first dynasty is believed to have been Qa'a, who probably lived between 3100 and 2090 BC. We cannot be absolutely sure where he was buried, but it was probably at Abydos. Confusion has arisen in that Qa'a's burial place, known as Tomb Q, is also associated with the first pharaoh of the second dynasty, Hetepsekhemwy, though it is possible that Hetepsekhemwy was responsible only for completing the construction of Qa'a's tomb.

The names of the first three rulers of the second dynasty were found inscribed on the back of a statue of a priest, confirming that Reneb and then Ninetjer followed Hetepsekhemwy. Hetepsekhemwy means 'pleasing in powers', but his tomb has not been found. It has been suggested that, in the interim, there were other kings who may have ruled.

Reneb, who probably ruled for some 39 years, succeeded Hetepsekhemwy. His predecessor had reunited lands in parts of Egypt after rebellions, leading us to believe that Reneb ruled during a peaceful period in Egypt's history. We do not know where he was buried, and his tomb could be either at Abydos or Saqqara. Reneb was succeeded by Ninetjer, but we do not know the relationship between the two.

Ninetjer's name means 'he who belongs to the god', and of all the kings of the second dynasty, he is the one we know most about. There are three tombs at Saqqara

LEFT: The Great Sphinx at Giza, illuminated as part of a son et lumière event.

OPPOSITE: Entrance to the temenos wall, Saqqara.

that bear his seal, and further seals have been found near Giza. At some point towards the end of his reign there was a period of unrest and it is probable that when he died, Egypt was going through a civil war, which probably led to three rulers controlling various parts of Egypt. Their names were probably Weneg, Sened and Nubnefer, but his true successor was Peribsen, also known as Seth-Peribsen.

Peribsen's name is significant, because it suggests that the followers of Set, or Seth, had gained supremacy over those of Horus. Peribsen had originally ascended the throne bearing the name of Sekhemib, but his name was changed so that he could associate himself with Set rather than Horus, the unrest between the followers of Set and Horus indicating the rivalry between Upper and Lower Egypt. The kings of the first and early part of the second dynasties are most closely associated with northern Egypt, whereas those of the latter part of the second dynasty have closer links with the south.

It is probable that Seth-Peribsen ruled for around 17 years, and he was buried in a fairly modest tomb at Abydos. Unfortunately, due to the fact that the burial chamber had been lined with mud bricks, only part of the structure remains.

Seth-Peribsen's successor was originally Khasekhem, but he changed his name to Khasekhemwy. This new name means 'the two powerful ones appear' and was an attempt to unite the Set and Horus factions, which indeed it did, when he crushed the rebellion and reunited Egypt. This pharaoh presided over huge building projects, including a monumental royal tomb at Abydos, as well as other constructions at El-Kab and Hierakonopolis. His most

impressive construction is known as the Shunet el-Zebib, or the storehouse of the dates, and is situated about 3,280ft (1,000m) from his royal tomb at Abydos. The tomb was of a mud-brick construction and was originally part of a huge complex of buildings. His style of constuction suggests they were forerunners of step pyramids and are therefore of importance in Egyptian architecture. It is believed that Khasekhemwy died around 2686 BC.

The death of Khasekhemwy heralded the beginning of the third dynasty and the rule of Sanakhte. Considerable mystery surrounds this king and it may be that he was in fact called Nebka and that he had usurped the rightful pharaoh, Netjerykhet Djoser. He may have reigned for periods of either five to seven years or 18 to 19. Details of his reign are missing from the Palermo Stone, but mention of him has been found on the island of Elephantine and in the Sinai Peninsula. In one relief, he is depicted wearing the red crown of Lower Egypt, and it is possible that he was the brother of his successor, Djoser. Sankhte's tomb was possibly incorporated into the Step Pyramid of the Pharaoh Djoser.

OPPOSITE: Pharaoh Djoser's Step Pyramid, Saqqara.

RIGHT & PAGE 108: The Colossi of Memnon once flanked the entrance to Amenhotep III's mortuary temple, but now stand virtually alone at the side of a road leading to the Valley of the Kings.

PAGE 109: Relief from the Temple of Seti I, Abydos.

Djoser was probably the most famous ruler of the third dynasty. His full name means 'the divine of body', and he probably ruled for around 19 years. He was responsible for building a large complex at Saqqara. He also organized several expeditions into the Sinai to defeat local Bedouin tribes and established turquoise mines at Wadi Maghara, also in Sinai. It was Djoser who commissioned the Step Pyramid at Saqqara, which was the first major monumental building to be constructed of stone.

His successor, Sekhemkhet, came to power in 2611 BC, and is variously depicted wearing both a white and a red crown. There is a debate as to how long he ruled, but it seems it could have exceeded seven years. Like his predecessor, he employed the architect, high priest, doctor and scribe, Imhotep, who had masterminded the construction of the Step Pyramid for Djoser.

The new king built another pyramid, which was uncovered at Saqqara shortly before the Second World War, and is now known as the Buried Pyramid of Sekhemkhet. It was built directly onto rock, which necessitated rough terrain being levelled, and may originally have been designed to have six or seven steps. Many artefacts were discovered inside the pyramid, including animal bones, papyri, stone vessels and golden artefacts, including bracelets. It was a remarkable find in a complex structure, considering it was only the second pyramid ever to have been built in Egypt.

OPPOSITE: The mortuary temple of Seti I at Luxor.

RIGHT: A stele from the temple of Seti I, depicting Re-Harakhte, a union of the deities Re and Harakhte (Horus), and personifying the morning sun.

was because Djedefre had seized the throne for himself by murdering his older half-brother, Kauab, who had had a better claim to the throne, being the son of a more prominent royal wife. There is considerable debate as to where Djedefre is buried, but it was probably in a pyramid at Abu Rawash.

Khafre (Chephren), having either murdered his half-brother or succeeded Kauab following Kauab's natural death, came to power in approximately 2520 BC. His name means 'appearing like Re', and he was responsible for the building of the second pyramid on the Giza plateau. The length of his rule has been variously calculated as between 24 and 66 years, which would suggest he was a relatively young man when he came to the throne. Most interesting is the fact that part of his will has been found, in which he leaves 14 towns to his heirs. Confusingly, 11 of the beneficiaries also went by the name of Khafre.

Many Egyptologists believe Khafre was responsible for the building of the Great Sphinx. This monumental statue of a lion with a human head is situated to the north-east of Temple Valley, in a location that was once a quarry. Here a huge U-shaped ditch was dug to isolate a massive block of rectangular bedrock, and it was from this enormous lump of limestone that the sphinx was crafted.

Sure enough, one of Khafre's heirs managed to succeed him in approximately 2472 BC. Menkaure (Mycerinus) is best known as the builder of the so-called Third Pyramid at Giza, in which archeologists were to discover slate statues and many other valuable objects. Menkaure's name means 'eternal like the souls of Re', and he probably had three queens, one of whom was his elder sister. His eldest son, Khuenre,

died before Menkaure and it was subsequently the younger son, Shepseskaf, who succeeded his father. Menkaure's son probably completed the pyramid and it was expanded later, suggesting that Menkaure's cult enjoyed a new burst of popularity during the fifth and sixth dynasties.

The name of the final king of the fourth dynasty, Shepseskaf, means 'his soul is noble'. He was probably the son of one of his father's minor queens, and his rule was short, at around four years. He did not choose to build a pyramid for his own tomb but instead ordered the construction of a *mastaba* in southern Saqqara, which was nevertheless huge, at nearly 330ft long and almost 250ft wide (100 x 75m). It consisted of two levels of large limestone blocks, the same material that came out of the quarries to the west of the pyramids at Dahshur.

The first ruler of the fifth dynasty and the successor to Shepseskaf was Userkaf, the grandson of Djedefre, whose name means 'his soul is powerful'. There does not seem to have been a major upheaval when he came to the throne, as several prominent officials of the fourth dynasty retained their positions. Perhaps the most significant contribution made by him was to make contact with civilizations in the Aegean. In fact, a stone vessel bearing his name was found on the island of Kythera.

Userkaf was almost certainly succeeded by his son, Sahure, in around 2458 BC, and he seems to have ruled for around 12 years. His name means 'he who is close

View of the Nile's left bank and the Aga Khan mausoleum, Aswan.

to Re'. His pyramid complex was built at Abusir and there was a considerable decline in its quality and size compared with the pyramids of the past. It is probable that Sahure created the Egyptian navy, indicated in scenes carved on stone vessels found in Libya. He built a sun temple, as did many of the other fifth-dynasty kings, and was succeeded by his brother, Neferirkare.

Neferirkare was the first pharaoh to have two names, though it was a custom that would be adopted by later kings. The throne name Neferirkare means 'beautiful is the soul of Re' and his birth name was Kakai. He probably only ruled for ten years. His pyramid remained unfinished and was ultimately incorporated into the pyramid complex built by Niuserre. In it, a papyrus was found detailing guard-duty rosters, offerings, and details of ceremonies.

It is not known how the next king, Shepseskare, was related to the other kings of the fifth dynasty, but he probably reigned for about seven years. The only physical evidence of his existence is an unfinished pyramid located at Abusir, between Userkaf's solar temple and Sahure's pyramid.

Of the next king we know rather more: his name was Neferefre and he was probably a son of Neferirkare Kakai. What is puzzling, however, is that he possibly came to the throne at a young age and his consort, Queen Khentkaus II, therefore acted as regent. But the body found in his pyramid at Abusir is of a man in his early 20s, and since he only ruled for two or

LEFT: A relief showing Mandulis, a Nubian god, in the Temple of Kalabsha, Aswan.

OPPOSITE: The kiosk of Qertassi, Kalabsha.

three years, why would he have needed a regent to act on his behalf? There are also references to him as Neferre, meaning 'Re is beautiful', though his name was later changed to Neferefre, meaning 'Re is his beauty'. He possibly built a solar temple called Hetep-Re, though it has never been discovered, and he is thought to have died suddenly, before his pyramid complex could be completed.

Neferefre was succeeded by Niuserre, who probably ruled for around ten years. Niuserre was Neferefre's younger brother and as pharaoh was involved in military campaigns, both in Sinai and in Libya. He constructed a valley temple, pyramid, and mortuary complex at Abusir, and also constructed a solar temple half a mile or so to the north. This temple is one of the biggest and most complete and is the only one made entirely of stone. It must have been a prosperous period for Egypt, because even high officials buried at this time were given large and ornate tombs.

The relationship of the seventh ruler of Egypt's fifth dynasty to his predecessors is also unclear. He could easily have been either a brother or a son of Niuserre, and his mother was probably Neput-Nebu, Niuserre's chief queen. The name of this king was Menkauhor Kalu, his first name meaning 'eternal are the souls of Re'. He was either the brother or the father of Djedkare, who succeeded him, and probably ruled for around eight years, from approximately 2421 to 2414 BC. He built a solar temple called Akhet-Re, which was probably located either at Saqqara or Abusir. He has associations with the so-called Headless Pyramid, located in north Saqqara.

The next king, Djedkare, had a principal queen called Meresankh IV. Her tomb is located at the centre of the Saqqara necropolis, though there is another pyramid of a wife or consort next to Djedkare's own pyramid in south Saqqara. Djedkare probably ruled for a period of between 28 and 38 years, his mummy revealing a man of around 50 years of age. His name means 'soul of Re endureth', but his birth name was Isesi. He did not build a sun temple, for there were important developments during his rule; by then the solar cult had lost much of its influence, and central government had relinquished some of its control to provincial administrators.

The final king of the fifth dynasty was Unas, who had a long reign and two principal queens – Khenut and Nebit – both of whom were buried in *mastaba* tombs near Unas's own pyramid complex at Saqqara. During his reign he encouraged trade, enjoyed hunting, and authorized building projects at Elephantine and Saqqara. He was also involved in some military campaigns. Unas's is one of the smallest of the royal pyramids built during the Old Kingdom period, and he is identified with the gods Re and Osiris. Parts of his mummy were discovered in 1880 and are now housed in the Cairo museum. He seems to have had a son, Ptahshepses, at one stage, but it is probable that he died before his father, which gave rise to a period of instability before Teti, the first pharaoh of the sixth dynasty, came to the throne.

Teti was also known as Seheteptawy, which means 'he who pacifies the two lands', suggesting he ruled a united Egypt. It is probable he came to power in 2345 BC and may have ruled for a little over 30 years. His wife was Queen Iput I, who was a daughter of Unas, which legitimized Teti's power. He had other wives, including Khuit and Weret-Imtes. Iput I is buried in her own pyramid close to that of Teti at Saqqara. Teti was the first pharaoh to be closely associated with Hathor, who was the mistress of heaven and goddess of love, music and beauty. She was also known as the mistress of life or the great, wild cow.

Teti was murdered by his guards, though we do not know the reason why, and his son succeeded him as Pepi I. Pepi I's other name was Meryre, which means 'beloved of Re', but he preferred to use another name during the first half of his reign, that of Nefersahor, and may have ruled for between 40 and 50 years. It is possible that Pepi did not follow his father directly in the line of succession, but that a usurper, by the name of Userkare, reigned for a short period of time. Nevertheless Pepi I went on to produce the two other kings of the sixth dynasty, Merenre Nemtyemzaf and Pepi II. Pepi I led campaigns against Palestine, initiated trade and exploratory expeditions, and masterminded several major building projects.

As the oldest living son of Pepi I, Merenre ('beloved of Re') was relatively young when he came to the throne, his mother being Ankhnesmerire I. Merenre married Ankhnesmerire II, another of his father's wives and the mother of his half-brother, Pepi II. This meant that Pepi II was Merenre's half-brother, stepson and cousin.

Egypt ruled as far south as the third cataract by this stage, and much of Nubia had been conquered. Merenre's mummy was buried in a pyramid in southern Saqqara, and because it was never quite completed, his death may have been unexpected.

Merenre was succeeded by Pepi II, who came to the throne at the age of six. Egyptologists cannot agree as to the length of time he reigned, however; some say

64 years, others 94. Pepi II's other name was Neferkare, which means 'beautiful is the soul of Re'. During his reign he established links with a number of other civilizations, including some in Southern Africa, and established strong commercial and diplomatic relations in parts of Syria and Palestine. He launched more campaigns in Nubia, with the intention of pacifying local tribes.

It seems that Egypt's wealth and power during this period lay in the hands of senior officials, who were able to build huge, elaborate tombs for themselves. Pepi II's tomb is relatively modest, decorated less richly than those of many of his predecessors. It seems that parts of the country were looking for semi-independence and it was Pepi II who appointed viziers to control Upper and Lower Egypt.

It is possible that Pepi II was succeeded by his son, Merenre II, but that he probably only lasted a year. After the end of Pepi II's rule, major building projects were put on hold until the 11th dynasty and the reign of Mentuhotep II.

The era spanned by the seventh, eighth, ninth, tenth and 11th dynasties, that followed Pept II's reign, is known as the Intermediate Period, which was when many of the kings' reigns overlapped and Egypt was no longer a unified state. When Mentuhotep II finally came to the throne in 2055 BC it was something of a renaissance for the country; not only did he re-establish order, he also sparked the beginning of enormous building projects in Egypt.

An artist's impression of the inside of the Dendera temple, by David Roberts, c.1840.

Chapter Four
THE LATER PHARAOHS

CHAPTER FOUR
THE LATER PHARAOHS

A succession of pharaohs followed Pepi II, whose reigns overlapped and of whom very little is known. The Middle Kingdom period began with the rise of Mentuhotep II, who could well have been the son or heir of Intef III, of the 11th dynasty. Known also as Nebhepetre, or 'pleased is the lord Re', Mentuhotep ruled Egypt from Thebes, which up to then had not been a particularly prominent city. Mentuhotep's principal wife was Tem, and he had at least two other wives, one of whom, Henhenet, died in childbirth, the other, Neferu, being the mother of his heir to the throne.

At first, Mentuhotep was not the ruler of a united Egypt, but it was during his reign that Upper and Lower Egypt eventually came together. This had not been easy to achieve and we know that there was a revolt at Abydos in the 14th year of his rule, which he had been quick to crush. It is probable that the unification of Egypt was not achieved until the 39th year of Mentuhotep's rule, which subsequently allowed him to launch military campaigns into Nubia. By the end of his 50-year reign, however, peace and prosperity had returned to Egypt and major building projects had begun. His greatest achievement was the temple and tomb he built for himself at Thebes, in what is now modern-day Luxor.

Mentuhotep III inherited a strong and prosperous country from his father, though by the time he became pharaoh in 2010 BC he was already an old man by contemporary standards and would only rule for 12 years. His name means 'the god Mentu is content' (Mentu being a solar or war god), but his throne name was Sankhkare, which means 'giving life to the soul of Re'. Mentuhotep III continued the good work of his predecessor, extending trade, defending Egypt's frontiers and building fortresses. He initiated a number of expeditions to obtain the raw materials for a comprehensive building programme, which included new temples and shrines. He also commissioned artworks, including portraits and fine stone carvings.

This was a positive time for Egypt, despite the famine that occurred in the area around Thebes, towards the end of Mentuhotep III's reign. His mortuary temple was not completed and he was probably buried in the cliffs at Deir el-Bhari, next to

FAR LEFT: Mentuhotep I was a local ruler or vizier in 11th-dynasty Thebes.

OPPOSITE: The 2nd-century BC Temple of Debod, given to Spain in 1968, and reconstructed in Madrid.

Queen Hatshepsut's temple, with several of his own high officials, including his chancellor, buried close by.

It is possible that a usurper was his successor, because Mentuhotep IV was not related by blood to the royal family. His name is missing from the king lists and he probably reigned for only around six years. Mentuhotep IV was also known as Nebtawyre, meaning 'lord of the two lands is Re', but more than that, not much else is known, and his tomb has never been found. He was also overthrown by a man not of the blood royal – Amenemhet I.

Amenemhet I, the first pharaoh of the 12th dynasty, had probably been Mentuhotep IV's vizier, and even though he had no real claim to the throne, he ruled Egypt for nearly 30 years. His Horus name was Wehemmesut, which means 'he who repeats births'. His mother was probably Nefret, from Elephantine, and his father was possibly a priest called Senusret (Sesostris), therefore his origins lay in southern Egypt. He decided to shift his capital to the south of Memphis, though the ruins of his city have never been discovered. At first, he began a tomb for himself at Thebes, but abandoned it to begin construction of a pyramid at El-Lisht. Aside from his own pyramid, he also authorized the building of fortresses, public buildings at Karnak, a temple to Mut, additions to a temple at Abydos, and yet another temple at Memphis. He probably worshipped Mentu, the god of war, rather than Amun, the principal god of Thebes. Amenemhet I was assassinated in a harem plot, while his son was away fighting in Libya.

After the murder of Amenemhet I, his son, Senusret I, whose mother was probably Neferytotenen, his father's senior wife, took the name of Kheperkare, meaning 'the soul of Re comes into being'. Senusret married Queen Nefru and together they produced a son who would become Amenemhet II; Senusret had already established a co-regency with his son, to ease him into his future role of pharaoh. He also had a number of daughters, some of whom may have died before their father.

Senusret I probably ruled for around 34 years, his life coming to an end in 1911 BC. His reign had been a period of affluence and stability for Egypt, which had grown famous not only for its mineral wealth, gold, and fine jewellery, but also for the amethyst, turquoise, copper and gniess that were applied to works of art; many such pieces have been found, particularly in the tombs of royal ladies at Dahshur and Lahun.

Senusret I continued many of his father's policies, in particular making forays into northern Nubia to establish greater control over the southern parts of the River Nile. He continued to build fortresses and by the end of his reign had constructed 13, which extended as far as the second cataract of the Nile. Military campaigns were launched into Libya, but trade and strong diplomatic relations were preferred as far as Syria and Palestine were concerned. It is believed that Senusret I worshipped Osiris, because the cult of the god greatly increased during his reign. Several building projects were established at Karnak and Heliopolis, he

OPPOSITE: The goddess Sekhmet, from the Temple of Mut, now in the Luxor museum.

RIGHT: Statue of Amun in Karnak's hypostyle hall.

remodelled the temple at Abydos, created new temples from Alexandria down to Aswan, and even extended into Nubia. In fact, monuments were built at all of the main cult sites in Egypt. Senusret I's own pyramid is located a little to the south of his father's at El-Lisht.

When Amenemhet II came to the throne in around 1911 BC he assumed the name Nubkaure, meaning 'golden are the souls of Re', the meaning of his own name being 'Amun is at the head'. Trading and establishing good diplomatic relationships were of paramount importance during Amenemhet II's reign. He exchanged gifts with many rulers in the Mediterranean and artefacts sent by the pharaoh have been found as far afield as Lebanon; there is also evidence of Egyptian contact with Crete, in that Kamares pottery, made at Knossos, has been discovered in a tomb at Abydos. The pharaoh also ordered military campaigns against the Bedouin in the Sinai, and expeditions were made into southern Nubia and the East African kingdom of Punt. During his reign, prominent administrators were allowed to pass their jobs onto their offspring, a practice that his predecessors, who had used personal appointments as a means of centralizing the state, had avoided in the past. Amenemhet II did not go in for a great deal of building. His own pyramid is at Dahshur and contains both ancient designs and some new ideas.

The fourth king of the 12th dynasty, Senusret II, came to the throne in approximately 1877 BC. His name means 'man of the goddess Wosret', but his throne name was Khakheperre, or 'the soul of Re comes into being'. He is shown as having a mobile face, with distinctive, broad cheekbones, and wide, muscular shoulders. His principal wife was

Khnumetneferhedjetweret; we know her name because her body was found in a tomb under the pyramid of her own son, Senusret III, who was Senusret II's successor. It was another peaceful time for Egypt, when trade with the Near East was flourishing, Egypt's mineral interests had increased, and it had acquired more territory in Nubia. Cultivation was expanding through various irrigation projects, which included the building of dykes and the construction of new canals. Senusret II built his pyramid close to the Fayoum Oasis at Lahun, starting a new trend by concealing the door in the pavement to the south side of the structure. There is also a sphinx, now in the museum in Cairo, that is believed to bear his likeness.

We know more about Senusret III, who probably came to power in around 1836 BC, than any other Middle Kingdom ruler. There are a great many statues showing him as a man with heavy eyelids and a lined face; this is believed to have been a common device used by artists to suggest a serious and thoughtful person. His throne name was Khakhaure, meaning 'appearing like the souls of Re', and he was buried along with his mother in a pyramid at Dahshur. His principal queen was Mereret, possibly also his sister, who probably outlived her husband.

Senusret III is thought to have been a man of over 6ft 6in (1.98m) tall, so his reputation as a great warrior

FAR LEFT: Hatshepsut (defaced) and Amun-Re, Deir el-Bahri, Luxor.

OPPOSITE: The relocated temple of Beit al-Wali, House of the Governor, at Kalabsha, Aswan.

is hardly surprising. In fact his imain aim was to establish even more control over Nubia, and he launched a series of campaigns early in his reign, continuing to do so almost every other year. Gradually, he began to gain control of the area, ordering the building of more fortresses than any of the other rulers of the Middle Kingdom had achieved before him. The eight fortresses were constructed along the 40-mile (64-km) stretch of the River Nile, from Semna to Buhen; treasures acquired during his campaigns in Nubia and Syria were also used to decorate temples, and they were refurbished using more costly materials. Large numbers of priests of Amun surrounded the pharaoh at his court at Thebes and a huge temple near Karnak was built, dedicated to the war god Mentu.

Domestically, Senruset, though determined to retain control, split the country into three administrative regions, appointing a council to preside over each, which reported to him via a vizier. The pharaoh had his own pyramid built at Dahshur, but was never buried there; instead, he was probably entombed in a vast complex stretching for over half a mile between the high desert cliffs and the edge of the Nile floodplain in southern Abydos.

Amenemhet III was the last of the great rulers of the Middle Kingdom. His chief wife bore the name of Aat, and she and others of his principal wives were buried in their own chambers in his pyramid.

When the pharaoh ordered the building of his pyramid at Dahshur, which took nearly 15 years to complete, it almost immediately began to collapse, with the result that a second pyramid was constructed at Hawara, allowing him to site his tomb closer to the region he loved. There was other building activity

going on in the region, including the construction of a temple to Sobek. He also built the temple at Quban in Nubia, and extended the Temple of Ptah in Memphis, while other temples and structures received his personal supervision. His successor, Amenemhet IV, was either his son or grandson.

Amenemhet IV came to power when he was already old and no heir was conceived. He was succeeded by his sister, Neferusobek, who took control of Egypt in 1763 BC. Her alternative name was Sobekneferu, which means 'the beauties of Sobek', the

crocodile god; a centre already existed at Fayoum, where crocodiles were bred and worshipped. She

OPPOSITE: Beit al-Wali, Kalabsha, another of Ramesses II's monuments to Amun.

FAR LEFT: Amun, and what is left of the torso of Ramesses II, in the Luxor museum.

ABOVE: Amun, the ram, flanked on either side by Apedemak, a lion god. National Museum, Khartoum.

Sekenenretao died suddenly during the war with the Hyksos, who had invaded Egypt and were causing immense disruption. Kamose continued the war against the Hyksos, riding in a chariot supported by his Nubian allies. He decisively defeated the Hyksos, then sailed up and down the Nile, searching for the Egyptians who had sided with the enemy. He died without issue and his brother, Ahmose I, succeeded him as pharaoh, becoming the first king of the 18th dynasty and the New Kingdom period. The 18th dynasty also includes Tutankhamun, who in reality was a fairly minor king. He achieved fame in modern times due to the fabulous treasures discovered in his tomb.

Ahmose I probably came to power when he was about ten years old, ruling for 25 years from 1550 BC. His own name means 'the moon is born', but his royal name was Nebpehtyre, 'the lord of strength is Re'. Later on in his reign, he attacked the Palestinian fortress of Sharuhen in a successful six-year siege, bringing to an end the Hyksos control of Egypt. Then he attacked Nubia, where he established new civil administrations; but while campaigning in the south, allies of the Hyksos made an attempt at rebellion, which his mother, Ahhotpe, successfully crushed in his absence. Ahmose I married his own sister and at least ten children were born. His tomb has never been found, though his mummy has come to light, found at Deir el-Bahri.

apparently ruled for around four years and was the last Egyptian ruler of the Middle Kingdom prior to the arrival of the Hyksos. She may well have been buried in one of the pyramids at Mazghuna, which is situated some 3 miles (5km) to the south of Dahshur. Whether or not this is the case remains a matter of conjecture, but her death led to what became known as the Second Intermediate Period, in which the kings of the 13th to the 17th dynasties struggled to control Egypt.

Eventually, members of the royal bloodline from Thebes managed to regain power, but in the meantime some 200 years would elapse before Kamose, the son of Sekenenretao and Queen Ahhotep, eventually came to the throne.

ABOVE LEFT: Relief of Sobek, the crocodile god, from the Temple of Sobek and Haroeris, Kom Ombo.

OPPOSITE: The mortuary temple of Tuthmose III, Karnak, with its sacred lake in the foreground.

Ahmose I was succeeded by his young son, Amenhotep I, who probably ruled for around 25 years. His name means 'Amun is pleased', but his throne name was Djeserkare, meaning 'holy is the soul of Re'. He was obliged to deal with a Libyan uprising during the first year of his reign, before turning his attention to Nubia and bringing back Nubian prisoners to Thebes. He organized the repair and restoration of many temples, the temple of Karnak, in Thebes, being one of his best-known projects. Some temples were expanded, particularly the ones connected with his father and mother. Amenhotep I was probably the first pharaoh to build his tomb some distance from his mortuary temple, possibly located at Dra Abu el-Naga, outside the Valley of the Kings. His son died in infancy, leaving his military commander, who had married Amenhotep's sister, to inherit the throne after his death.

The new pharaoh, Tuthmose I, was therefore a commoner and a soldier, his name meaning 'born of the god Thoth'. He launched a series of military campaigns that followed on from his work under the previous pharaoh. His troops penetrated beyond the third cataract and he fought against the Syrians and reached the Euphrates river. Meanwhile, his architect, Ineni, was building an extension to the Temple of Amun at Karnak, while other work was progressing at

OPPOSITE: This 26-ft (8-m) alabaster sphinx, dedicated to the god Ptah and thought to be a likeness of Amenhotep III, once flanked the temple at Memphis.

LEFT: Obelisk of Tuthmose I, Karnak.

Giza. Further building projects also took place at Elephantine, Memphis, Edfu, Qasr Ibrim and at a temple in the Sinai at Serabit el-Khadim. He had two sons, Wadjmose and Amenmose, but both died before him, and was also the father of a daughter, Hatshepsut, another future monarch. Fortunately, he had another son by a minor queen, who became Tuthmose II.

More than likely, Tuthmose I was buried in the Valley of the Kings; his mummy was probably moved some time after his death, during the reign of Tuthmose III.

Tuthmose II is thought to have been a physically weak man, and to legitimize his rule, married his half-sister, Hatshepsut, who became the main power behind the throne. He is thought to have died in his early 30s, having reigned for no more than 14 years, during which time he sent troops into Palestine and Nubia and authorized some fairly modest building projects. His mummy was found at Deir el-Bahri, but no tomb has, as yet, been discovered.

When Tuthmose II died in 1479 BC, his son by a minor wife, Tuthmose III, was appointed heir, though the real power still lay in the hands of Hatshepsut. Because the pharaoh was still young, Hatshepsut became his regent, and they ruled together for a number of years until she proclaimed herself pharaoh, possibly when Tuthmose III was reaching manhood. She managed to rule for about 20 years, before disappearing from history, when Tuthmose III became pharaoh in his own right.

Tuthmose III eventually became a great pharaoh, winning military victories and planning extensive campaigns. He famously took the city of Megiddo (Armageddon), seizing enormous riches in the process, fought a series of decisive battles in Syria, and established Egyptian dominance over Palestine. It is said that his military exploits led to the capture of 350 cities; during the 42nd year of his rule he captured Kadesh, and campaigns were also launched against the Nubians. He was also prolific in terms of building, constructing temples, rock sanctuaries and monuments, as well as the Festival Hall temple at Karnak. He is believed to have ruled for nearly 50 years and was eventually buried in the Valley of the Kings. His son, Amenhotep II, succeeded him as the seventh pharaoh of Egypt's 18th dynasty.

Amenhotep II was reputed to be an athlete, who trained horses and was an accomplished archer and charioteer. He made several military expeditions into Syria, bringing back enormous quantities of gold, copper, horses, chariots and prisoners. It was a peaceful time in Egypt and Nubia, which allowed him to complete many of the major sites his father had begun, and he left monuments, temples and other structures of his own to posterity. In a task began by his father, he also systematically eliminated all references to Hatshepsut's existence. He was buried in the Valley of the Kings, and until the discovery of Tutankhamun's tomb, Amenhotep's was the only mummy to have been found still in its sarcophagus.

Pharaoh Tuthmose IV probably came to the throne in 1419 BC, his throne name being Menkheperure, which means 'everlasting are the manifestations of Re'. His father had never recognized him as his successor, indicating that his claim to the throne may not have been legitimate. He nevertheless produced his own heir to the throne from his marriage with Mutemwiya, who was probably the daughter of the Mitannian king, Artatama, and he may also have married one of his own sisters. There was little military action during his reign and little is known concerning his building projects, though he did complete a large obelisk designed for the Temple of Karnak. The obelisk was supposed to be one of a pair, but the stone intended for it, that had been quarried at Aswan, was discovered to be faulty and was rejected. He authorized several other minor building projects around Egypt and in Nubia. His own tomb is in the Valley of the Kings, but his mummy was found missing when the tomb was investigated; it was found five years later, among a cache of mummies discovered in the tomb of Amenhotep II.

The son of Tuthmose IV became Amenhotep III and ruled Egypt for 40 years. Some refer to him as the Napoleon of Ancient Egypt, on account of his successful campaigns against Libya, Nubia and Syria. His throne name was Nubmaatre, meaning 'lord of truth is Re'. There are some wonderful images of his birth in the temple at Luxor and it is probable that he came to the throne when he was only two years old. He later acquired a large harem, mainly through diplomatic marriages. His eldest son died prematurely, with the result that Amenhotep IV, better known as Akhenaten, became his successor.

Amenhotep IV would eventually be known as the Heretic Pharaoh. He married Nefertiti, the daughter of his vizier, Ay, and introduced the monotheistic cult of the Aten, the worship of the sun represented by the

Tutankhamun's death mask, decorated with gold and semi-precious stones.

responsibility of governing Egypt with Ay and led failed expeditions against the Hittites, declaring himself king when Ay died, by which time he was middle-aged. He probably married the sister of Nefertiti, to cement his royal connections, and is thought to have ruled for around 27 years. He chose Paramesse as his heir, having no sons of his own. Horemheb was the last pharaoh of the 18th dynasty.

Paramesse would become Ramesses I and the grandfather of one of the greatest of the pharaohs, Ramesses II. Ramesses I had been a military commander, but he was not of the royal blood. His

OPPOSITE LEFT: Nefertari and Isis, a wall painting from Nefertari's tomb, Abu Simbel.

OPPOSITE RIGHT: Amenhotep III, from the Temple of Luxor, now in the Luxor museum.

RIGHT: The colossal statue of Ramesses II at Memphis is 43ft (13m) long and made from hard, fine-grained limestone.

PAGES 140–141: Temples of Ramesses II and Nefertari, dedicated to Re-Harakhte and Hathor, at Abu Simbel.

PAGE 142 LEFT: A papyrus showing Nefertari, the wife of Ramesses II.

PAGE 142 RIGHT: Detail showing Princess Benta-Anat at the feet of the statue of Ramesses II, Karnak.

PAGE 143: The Temple of Ramesses II at Abu Simbel.

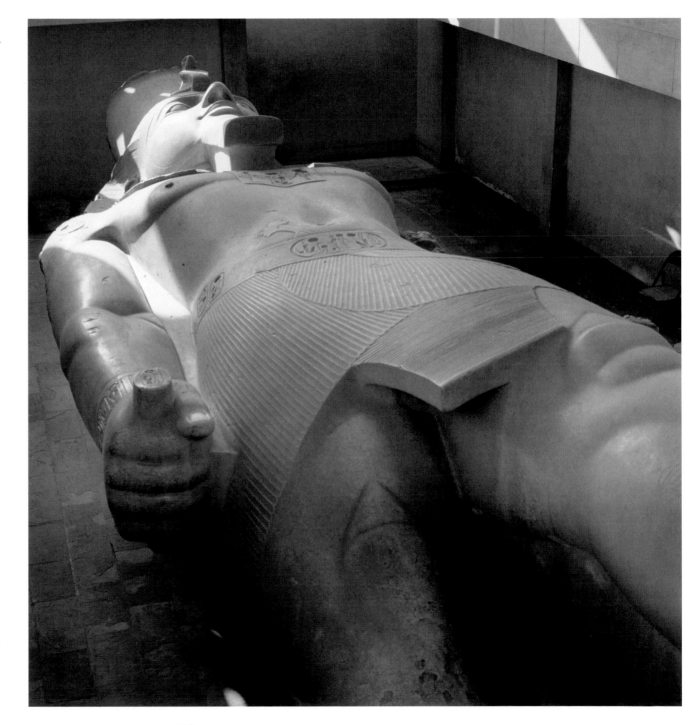

family came from the north-eastern part of the Nile delta and he had one son who would become Seti I. It is probable that Ramesses I only ruled Egypt for two years, so little construction work can be directly attributed to him. He was buried in a small tomb in the Valley of the Kings.

Seti I ruled Egypt for between 13 and 20 years from around 1394 BC. His first wife was Tuya, the daughter of his commander of chariots. Seti I launched campaigns into Palestine, Syria and Lebanon, and crushed a rebellion in Nubia. He ordered the beginning of the building of the hypostyle hall in the Temple of Amun at Karnak – a project that would be completed by his son. He also directed the building of a temple with seven sanctuaries at Abydos and another structure, known as the Osireion, built behind, below and connected to the Temple of Seti I, with a tunnel painted with scenes from the Book of Gates. One of his most impressive constructions was his own mortuary temple and tomb in the Valley of the Kings. It is one of the longest and deepest and was actually completed. His is one of the finest of all the surviving royal mummies, but it was not discovered in his own tomb, having been removed and taken to Deir el-Bahri instead.

Ramesses II (Ramesses the Great), also known as Usermaatresetepenre, is said to have lived to the ripe old age of 96, and from his 200 wives and concubines produced no less than 96 sons and 60 daughters. He was responsible for a number of building projects, including a mortuary complex at Abydos, a huge tomb at Thebes, extensions to the Luxor temple, the construction of the Colossus of Ramesses II, a vast statue carved in limestone, and the building of the

Ramesseum, a mortuary temple on the site of Seti I's ruined temple at Luxor. Ramesses II was a major military leader, often depicted capturing and slaughtering his enemies. He expanded Egypt's territories and led the Egyptian army against the Hittites at the Battle of Kadesh. Whether or not this was the crushing victory Ramesses II claimed, is a source of conjecture, but certainly the Hittites were greatly weakened by the experience. Ramesses II was succeeded by his 13th son, having already outlived the previous 12.

When Merenptah became pharaoh in around 1213 BC, he was already 60 years old and did not last for more than ten years. In fact this pharaoh had been virtually unknown until about 40 years into his father's reign. By this stage, Merenptah had become a military leader and was officially made heir to the throne on his father's 80th birthday. He quelled revolts in both Libya and Nubia, but otherwise tried to maintain peaceful relations with his neighbours. He moved the administrative centre of Egypt to Memphis, where he also built a royal palace. He probably died in around 1202 BC, though his mummy was never found. There are two theories concerning the reason for this; either he was the pharaoh in the Bible's Exodus, and was therefore washed away into the Red Sea, or his body was one of the 18 mummies found in the tomb of Amenhotep II.

Queen Nefertari's temple at Abu Simbel.

The next king, Amenmesses, was probably not the legitimate heir to the throne, being the son of Merenptah, but not by a prominent wife. He only ruled for three years or so and his incomplete tomb is located in the Valley of the Kings.

A legitimate ruler, in the person of Seti II, now became pharaoh, ruling for only six years. It was a period of relative peace in Egypt and only minor construction work was begun, due to the short span of his reign. His tomb in the Valley of the Kings must have lain open for many years, having been heavily defaced with Greek and Latin graffiti, which have since been removed.

The next king was Siptah, who is believed to have had a club foot. Again, it was a short reign of possibly six years, and he, too, was buried in the Valley of the Kings.

There were obvious problems regarding the succession, as the last pharaoh of the 19th dynasty was in fact a queen, Tausert – the great wife of Seti II. Little is known concerning her rule and her mummy has never been positively identified.

Setnakhte became the first pharaoh of the 20th dynasty. He was probably not of royal blood, but had helped Tausert to rule Egypt. His other name was Airsu, literally meaning 'self-made man', which would infer he had usurped the throne. He ruled for only two or three years and was probably of advanced years when he became king.

The Abu Simbel temples and Lake Nasser.

There now came a succession of pharaohs, all named Ramesses, who ruled from 1184 to 1069 BC. Ramesses III, the first of these, was destined to produce the next three rulers of Egypt, Ramesses IV, Ramesses V and Ramesses VI. This was a period of consolidation for Egypt. There were wars against the Libyans and a new threat had arisen to fill the vacuum created by the fall of the Hittite empire. This came in the shape of the Sea Peoples, invaders of uncertain identity from the eastern Mediterranean. All of these rulers fought the Sea Peoples in an attempt to prevent them from making incursions into the region.

Ramesses VII was probably the son of Ramesses VI, but all we know of him is his tomb in the Valley of the Kings and that he produced a son who failed to survive him. Therefore Ramesses VIII was the son of Ramesses III. His mummy has never been found and little is known concerning his rule.

We are even less sure of Ramesses IX, even though he ruled for at least 17 years. His son did not outlive him, which opened the way for Ramesses X, another king shrouded in mystery, although he does have a tomb in the Valley of the Kings.

The last king of the New Kingdom period was Ramesses XI. We know very little of him, though he did manage to reign for around 28 years. There were still problems with the Libyans during his reign and

OPPOSITE: Statue of Ramesses II, Karnak.

LEFT: Osiride pillars in the portico of the temple of Ramesses III at Karnak.

there were undoubtedly some revolts in Egypt. When Ramesses XI died in 1069 BC, Egyptian history entered what is known as the Third Intermediate Period.

From around 1070 through to 747 BC, there were different rulers in the north and south and some pharaohs may only have controlled portions of Egypt, with the capital moving to and from various locations around the country. By the time of the 25th dynasty and the rule of Piye, the situation had become thoroughly confused.

Piye had ascended the Nubian throne when he made advances into Egypt, eventually consolidating his control of both Nubia and Egypt. When Piye died, he was buried at El-Kurru, in a small pyramid.

We know far more about Egypt's second Nubian ruler, Shabaka, believed to be the father or the uncle of his immediate successor, Shebitku. Shabaka is believed to have been Piye's younger brother. He established himself at Memphis, where he organized the construction of cult centres to the god Amun. Eventually he was buried, like Piye, in a steep-sided pyramid in Nubia, at El-Kurru.

The next pharaoh was Shabaka's nephew or son, Shebitku. By now the Assyrians were overrunning parts of the Middle East and it was a dangerous time for Egypt. Shebitku was succeeded by his brother, Taharqa. The Assyrians now invaded Egypt, capturing

OPPOSITE: Further view of the portico of the temple of Ramesses III at Karnak.

LEFT: The first Court of Ramesses III, Medinet Habu, Luxor.

Memphis, wounding the pharaoh, and carrying off his family and property. Taharqa died in 664 BC and was succeeded by Tanwetamani, who was the last Nubian king of Egypt. We do not know how he was related to Taharqa.

Tanwetamani managed to craft a victory against the Assyrians and for a time was able to control large parts of Egypt; but it was only a matter of time before the Assyrians would be back. Confusingly, there was another ruler of Egypt at this time, called Psammetichus I, the first ruler of the 26th dynasty, who probably ruled the delta region of Egypt, while Tanwetamani controlled the southern half and Nubia. Eventually, in his ninth year of rule, Psammetichus gained complete control of all Egypt. But he was a pharaoh in name only, and prey to the whims of the Assyrian rulers. Gradually, however, he succeeded in raising an army to throw the Assyrians out of Egypt, which he eventually was able to achieve, allowing his son, Nekau II, to assume the throne.

Nekau (Necho) II was succeeded by Psammetichus II, and by this stage new building projects were under way. To cement his control over Nubia, the pharaoh also launched expeditions into Palestine, but a new danger was imminent, waiting to exploit Egypt's weakened situation. There would be only three more truly independent Egyptian pharaohs before the country was crushed beneath the yoke of the great Persian empire.

The first was Psammetichus II's son, Apries, who immersed himself in military operations and foolishly became involved in Libya's attempts to beat off the Greek invaders. His troops were badly beaten and a civil war broke out in Egypt.

The last great Egyptian pharaoh was Amasis, who came to power in 570 BC and probably ruled for 45 years. Amasis, formerly a military commander, sent to crush a revolt, was surprised when his soldiers made him pharaoh instead. He therefore began a campaign against his predecessor, Apries, defeating him in battle. His son would follow him as Psammetichus III, though he ruled for only a single year.

But unfortunately for Amasis and his son, the Persians were heading in their direction. The Persians captured Lydia in 546 BC, before overrunning Chaldea, but by the time the Persians had reached his border, Amasis was dead. His son was captured, and Cambyses II, officially of the 27th, or Persian dynasty, took control of Egypt as pharaoh.

OPPOSITE: One of the Colossi of Memnon, Luxor.

ABOVE: The Great Entry Portal to the Sanctuary of Dendera, by David Roberts, 1838.

RIGHT: Propylon gate (north gate), Dendera.

Chapter Five
EGYPTIAN GODS & CREATION MYTHS

in Egyptian mythology. Other myths developed, inspired by the gods and goddesses associated with every aspect of human life, such as Bes, the protector of the household, and Hathor, who represented motherhood and fertility.

Of importance to many Egyptians, and closely connected with Re, was the concept of *maat*, personified in the goddess Maat, who represented the order of the universe and without whom the whole of creation would perish. There was also a direct link between Maat and the pharaoh, in that it was the pharaoh's responsibility to maintain order, by ensuring that law and justice were correctly applied. Maat was believed to be ever-present, and her name was invoked whenever a correct and impartial judgement had to be made.

After death, in what was called the Weighing of the Heart, jackal-headed Anubis, the god of mummification and the protector of tombs, weighed the hearts of the dead, using scales counterbalanced by Maat's ostrich feather. If the heart outweighed the feather, then it was deemed heavy with evil deeds and the person's soul was fed to Ammit, the Great Devourer. If the scales balanced, however, the soul of the deceased was welcomed into the Blessed Land by Osiris himself. Maat's influence was so profound that

OPPOSITE: Chapel of the Union with the Disk, on the roof of the Temple of Hathor at Dendera.

ABOVE RIGHT: Anubis, wearing a jackal's mask, from Hatshepsut's Anubis chapel at Deir al-Bahri, Luxor.

all believed that chaos would befall Egypt, should belief in her sacred tenets ever fail.

The pharaohs provided the essential link between the gods and the Egyptian people, and were often depicted making offerings to the gods. In addition to their personal name, Egyptian pharaohs invariably adopted a special throne name, often connecting them with the god Re, for example, and were regarded as his

offspring; they became personifications of the god Osiris when they died. In theory, the pharaoh presided over all ceremonies and rites, but since this was not practical, others were delegated to take his place.

The Ancient Egyptians believed there was a time when nothing existed. The priests of the sun god, Atum, developed what is known as the Ennead of Heliopolis, that comprised nine great gods: Atum, Shu,

Aker was an earth god, the guardian and gatekeeper of the Underworld. He is represented by the sign for the horizon, with a lion's head at both ends. The Egyptians believed that during the night the sun travelled through a tunnel, guarded at each end by a lion. It was believed that Aker opened earth's gate, so that Re could pass into the Underworld.

Am-heh was another god of the Underworld, whose name means 'devourer of millions'. He is said

ABOVE: Maat, Lady of Truth, Order and Justice. The Metropolitan Museum of Art, New York.

RIGHT: Maat (above), in the tomb of Queen Nefertari at Abu Simbel.

OPPOSITE LEFT: A modern mural from the west bank, Luxor, depicting the jackal-headed god Anubis.

OPPOSITE RIGHT: The Anubis chapel in the mortuary temple of Queen Hatshepsut, Deir el-Bahri.

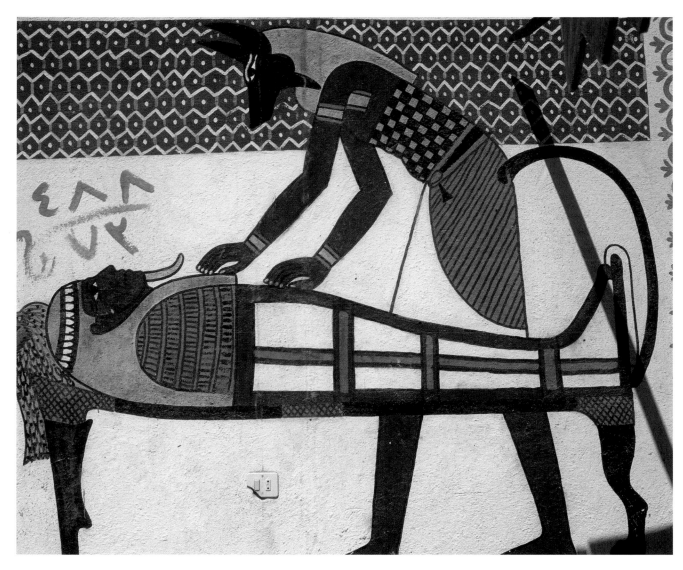

to have had the face of a hunting dog. and to have inhabited a lake of fire. The only god capable of dealing with him was Atum.

Yet another Underworld god was **Ament**, Aken's mate, often shown as a woman dressed as a queen. It was her function to greet the souls of the newly-dead, and bring them bread and water.

As already mentioned, the hideous demon **Ammit** was the devourer of the souls of the wicked. Ammit could be seen, crouched beneath the scales of justice in front of the throne of Osiris. Once the soul had been weighed and found wanting, the soul of the deceased would be fed to Ammit, resulting in the total annihilation of the person.

Apep was regarded as the personification of evil and darkness and was, in effect, an evil spirit. Each day. he attempted to devour Re's sun barque, as it sailed through the heavens. It was Set's role to prevent Apep from doing this, but occasionally Set failed and a so-called solar eclipse would occur. Apep was believed to resemble a giant serpent or crocodile, in command of a large army of demons. Each year, the priests of Re performed a ritual, known as the Banishing of Apep, in which they prayed that all the wickedness in Egypt would be absorbed into an effigy of the god, which they would then trample and burn, rendering Apep impotent for another year.

Astarte was a relative latecomer to the pantheon, having come to prominence during the 18th dynasty.

Originally a warrior goddess from Syria, she is sometimes shown wearing bulls' horns and, like Anat, was believed to be a daughter of Re and the wife of the god Set.

The **Aten** emerged during the New Kingdom, being the personification of the radiant disk of the sun. The Pharaoh Amenhotep IV (later Akhenaten) had a huge temple at Karnak built to this new god, who would become 'king of kings' and make the need for other gods disappear. This was to cause a major upheaval, as far as Egyptian worship was concerned, causing the other gods to slip into the cosmological background. It was probably as a result of political manoeuvrings that the Aten had come into being, enabling the power of the priesthood to be curtailed and allowing supreme power to be vested in the pharaoh himself. Because the Aten had been forced onto the Egyptian people, the other gods were never quite eliminated.

Atum was the prime mover, revered as the father of the gods and the father of the pharaohs. He is shown as a black bull, bearing the disk of the sun between his horns. Atum symbolized the setting sun and the sun's journey through the Underworld.

OPPOSITE: Relief symbolizing the goddess Mut, her vulture wings outstretched.

RIGHT: The goddess Isis, wife and sister of Osiris, from the Temple of Philae, Aswan.

PAGES 172–173: Trajan's kiosk at the Temple of Isis, Philae.

Horus is one of Egypt's better-known deities, though his attributes are somewhat complicated, and he was a sky-god in his original form. In fact, the Hor syllable of his name is associated with height or distance, representing the flight of the hunting falcon, when he became the lord of the sky. But Horus would ultimately be transformed into a sun god, in the guise of a falcon with outstretched wings. Now he was the god of the rising and setting sun, but particularly of the sunrise, in that he was reborn each day as the disk of the sun appeared in the east.

After Osiris was murdered by his brother, Set, Horus, the son of Osiris and Isis, fought Set for the throne of Egypt. Horus lost one of his eyes in the battle, which led to the remaining Eye of Horus being adopted as a powerful symbol of protection and power in Egypt. Horus is sometimes shown wearing the double crown of Egypt, having been responsible for uniting Egypt. He bestowed divinity on the pharaohs, many of whom took a Horus name under which they ruled. Horus was worshipped in many different forms and assimilated many other gods, being particularly associated with southern Egypt. In some quarters, the image of the Christian St. George slaying the dragon, is believed to have been synchretized from a depiction of Horus thrusting a spear into a serpent.

Hu was regarded as the voice of authority and the guardian of the spoken word. Along with Sia and the falcon-headed sun-god, Horus, Hu is often shown crossing the sky in a boat, signifying the recreation of the world as the sun rises each day. He also accompanied the pharaoh to the Afterlife after death, making sure the king retained his royal authority as he crossed the waters.

was the daughter of Nut and Geb, and the mother of Horus. In the early period, not only was she the sister of Osiris, but also his wife and female counterpart. According to the legend, after the death of Osiris at the hands of Set, Isis wandered through the world, collecting up the parts of Osiris's body that had been scattered to prevent him from being brought back to life. She was helped in her impossible task by Thoth, who also brought agriculture, magic and medicine to mankind. At some point, Isis was considered to be even more powerful than Re and Osiris, and was reputed to bring warmth and love, power and compassion to those who venerated her. Sometimes she is depicted as a woman with a solar disk on her head.

Mentu (Montu) was both a solar and a warrior god, who probably came to prominence in Thebes during the 11th dynasty. By the 12th dynasty, however, he had become subordinate to Amun and was relegated to the role of a god of war. By the 18th dynasty pharaohs, such as Tuthmose III, were beginning to refer to themselves as Mentu on the battlefield. Mentu also had connections with ordinary Egyptian households and was considered to be a protector of the home. He had cult centres at Armant, Madu, Tod and Karnak, and is depicted as a man with a falcon's head and a solar disk. He later became associated with the Buchis and Medamud bull cults, when he was depicted

It is believed that as Hu drew his first breath and each one thereafter, an act of creation occurred, his first breath creating the soul of Osiris and his last the sun. Importantly, it was believed in Ancient Egypt that the Great Sphinx of the Giza plateau was an image of Hu, in that it wore the red crown of the creator, its body symbolizing power and strength.

Isis is probably one of the oldest of the deities of Ancient Egypt, but she was been able to survive the generations very much in her original form. Isis was worshipped by many as a mother-goddess, seen as a protector and source of guidance and peace. There are many temples to Isis in Egypt, and she was even adopted by the Greeks and Romans in later times. She

OPPOSITE: Interior of the Temple of Re-Harakhte, Abu Simbel.

ABOVE LEFT: A depiction of Queen Nefertari and the god Horus in the tomb of Nefertari, Abu Simbel.

with the head of a bull. Later still, he became associated with Re, although he is sometimes paired with Atum and Set, and it is probable that the Greeks adopted him as their war god, Aries.

Mertseger is shown either as a woman with the head of a cobra or as a scorpion with a woman's head, and was worshipped by the workers who constructed the tombs in the Valley of the Kings. She was believed to inhabit the valley, living on a nearby mountain-top, where she was the protector and guardian of the tombs, sending poisonous creatures to attack anyone who had the temerity to disturb them. She was, however, merciful, and if transgressors repented, she would heal their wounds, making her both the goddess of punishment and of mercy.

Mut is depicted as a woman with vulture wings. Mut means mother, but she was regarded in Egypt as the grandmother to Isis's mother figure. Mut was the consort of Amun and their son was Khonsu, the moon god; they were worshipped as a trinity at Thebes. Mut eventually came to represent the mother of the pharaoh and was revered well into Roman times.

Nephthys, the sister of Osiris and Isis, was the wife of Set. She is often shown in a funeral boat, accompanying the dead on their way to the Blessed Land. She was regarded as the head of the household of the gods and is often shown standing at the beds of

LEFT: The Temple of Philae, viewed from the River Nile.

PAGE 178: A depiction of Osiris, from the tomb of Menna in the Valley of the Nobles, Luxor.

the royal boat from Apep. The original site of her veneration is thought to have been the Nile delta, but her cult eventually spread further afield. However, no temples dedicated to her have been discovered.

Set, or Seth, is usually depicted as a man with a jackal-like head, but when he is fighting Horus, he is shown as a hippopotamus, a black pig or occasionally a crocodile. The Egyptians regarded bright red as an evil colour, so he is also shown as a man with red hair and eyes, wearing a red mantle. Set was originally worshipped as a god of wind and desert storms, but at some point perceptions of him changed, when he was seen as a god of evil, engaged in an eternal conflict with Horus, the embodiment of the gods of light. By the 26th dynasty, Set had become the very essence of evil, and his worshippers abandoned him for Re and Osiris. In the legend of Osiris, Set kills Osiris, claiming the throne of the gods for himself; it is left to Horus to restore order by killing him.

Shesmu was an Ancient Egyptian demon god and the god of the wine press. It is said that he tore the heads of wrongdoers from their bodies, throwing them

OPPOSITE: Columns in the Temple of Sobek and Haroeris, Kom Ombo.

.

RIGHT: Relief of Sobek, guardian of the gods and pharaohs, Kom Ombo.

FAR RIGHT: Thoth, the god of wisdom, from the mortuary temple of Ramesses III at Medinet Habu.

PAGES 182–183: The Nile between Luxor and Dendera.

into a wine press and squeezing out their blood. He is sometimes depicted as a man with a lion's or a hawk's head. In the Pyramid Texts, Shesmu offers the pharaoh red wine or blood to refresh him on his travels. He was

also associated with the setting sun, possibly because red is the colour of blood. By the New Kingdom, however, Shesmu had became the god of the oil press, and of the precious oils used in beauty treatments, embalming and temple rituals. He was also the focus of

FAR LEFT: Sobek and Amenhotep III, in the Luxor museum.

ABOVE & OPPOSITE: Temple of Sobek and Haroeris, Kom Ombo.

a priesthood dating back many generations, and there were cult centres to him at Fayoum, Edfu and Dendera.

Sia is one of a pair with the god Hu. He is often seen travelling in the boat of the sun god Re, having been created from Re's blood. It is unlikely that he ever

LEFT: The ibis-headed god Thoth.

ABOVE: Mayi Magistave making an offering to Sobek. From the Temple of Sobek in Dahamsha, and now in the Luxor museum.

OPPOSITE: Ramesses III and Thoth. Ramesses's mortuary temple, Medinet Habu.

had a cult following of his own, even though he was the personification of the perceptive mind.

Sobek, the crocodile god, who was worshipped throughout Egypt, was the son of Neith, a god of war and of weaving. He acted as a bodyguard to various gods, particularly Re and Set, and is believed to have protected the pharaohs from all harm, particularly evil magic. He is depicted as a crocodile-headed man wearing a feathered crown.

The name **Tatenen** probably means 'the rising earth or exalted earth' and the god is often depicted as human man. He is also shown wearing a twisted ram's horn with two ostrich plumes, and occasionally with sun disks on his head. His limbs are often painted green, indicating his role as a god of vegetation. As a creator god, he held the title 'father of the gods' and is closely associated with the god Ptah. By the New Kingdom he had assumed a protective role in respect of the royal dead, and was responsible for guiding their souls through the Underworld.

Thoth was the patron of writing, scribes, secrets, and knowledge. He is shown as a man with the head of an ibis, or occasionally as a full ibis or a baboon, and holds a scribe's palette and stylus. He may have been a son of Re or he may have created himself through the power of language. He is credited with the creation of writing and magic, and was a teacher, messenger,

OPPOSITE: Façade, with pylons and reliefs, of the Temple of Horus, Edfu.

LEFT: Min, god of fertility, from the Red Chapel of Hatshepsut and Tuthmose III. Open-Air Museum, Karnak.

189

mediator and record-keeper. It was Thoth who questioned the souls of the dead before their hearts are weighed. Although he was worshipped throughout Egypt, his cult centre was at Hermopolis.

Wadjet is shown as a rearing cobra and a protector of the pharaoh – also as a woman with the head of a cobra, as a winged cobra, or as a woman with a lion's head. In Lower Egypt she is shown wearing a red crown. She eventually became a goddess of heat and fire and is connected with several other deities. Besides being worshipped as a goddess, she was considered to be a part of the land of Egypt itself.

Yah was an Egyptian moon god, and controversy still rages concerning the similarity of his name to that of the early form of Yahweh, one of the Hebrew god's sacred names. Little is actually known of Yah's cult in Egypt, but he seems to have become popular during the

LEFT: The goddess Hathor, Hatshepsut's mortuary temple, Deir el-Bahri.

OPPOSITE: The Chapel of Hathor, Deir el-Bahri.

PAGES 192–193: View of the Temple of Nefertari and Hathor, Abu Simbel.

PAGE 194: The small Roman temple dedicated to the goddess Isis, Temple of Hathor, Dendera.

PAGE 195 LEFT: Figures in the temple of Re-Harakhte.

PAGE 195 RIGHT: Serqet, the scorpian goddess, from the tomb of Nefertari.

Middle Kingdom period, when Egypt was being influenced by deities from Palestine, Syria and Babylon.

Cults were many and various throughout Ancient Egypt – not all of them to do with worshipping the gods. There were private cults, animal cults, funerary cults and, of course, cults worshipping the king. The Egyptians considered the link between religion and the state to be crucial, which was how the pharaoh came to be considered divine. He was transformed into a god at his coronation, and as such became a son of Re, a manifestation of Horus, and was absorbed into the godhead of Osiris when he died.

Interestingly, and a reason for the difficulty in setting accurate dates, is the fact that an incoming pharaoh would sometimes occupy the throne before the ruler he replaced had died: when this happened, the previous pharaoh would be treated as a manifestation of the god Osiris, even though he was still alive.

Royal cults came to particular prominence during the New Kingdom, when devotees were expected to make offerings to large statues of the kings, which the kings themselves had erected. Indeed, the kings were often depicted making offerings to their own god-like selves.

The Temple of Luxor, begun during the Middle Kingdom, was a monument to the divine, living king, and offerings to his spirit continued after his death.

OPPOSITE: Kiosk of Trajan, Philae, Aswan.

LEFT: Tomb painting in the Temple of Seti I, showing the king and the god Wepwawet, the Lord of Abydos.

PAGES 198–199: Lake Nasser at Abu Simbel.

The Step Pyramid of Djoser is a prime example of the role of the king in the Afterlife, in that it was meant to symbolize a royal palace, where the king could rule for all eternity. Mortuary temples attracted funerary cults and were regarded as places of great importance.

It should not be forgotten that the power and symbolism of the pharaoh grew in proportion to the development of religion in Egypt. The pharaoh was seen as a leader who protected his people. Moreover, he was ultimately responsible for making good any shortfall in the food supply, even to the extent of capturing food by military means, should the harvest fail.

Ultimately, all of the pharaoh's activities were seen as being in accordance with the will of the gods. Thus Egyptians would thank the gods for allowing them to take food from their neighbours, while the pharaoh would be also blessed for providing a plentiful harvest. It follows, therefore, that the king was seen as divine, which in theory, ruled out any challenge to his authority. The priests invariably supported the king, it being in their best interests to do so, but in the event of a scapegoat being needed, priests were blamed and

OPPOSITE LEFT: Painting of a guardian god of the Underworld in the Tomb of Sennedjem, Valley of the Queens, Deir el-Medina.

OPPOSITE RIGHT: Satis, goddess of the Nile's inundation, embracing a pharaoh. Yebu, Elephantine Island, Aswan.

LEFT: A Hathor-headed column, Chapel of the Union with the Disk, Dendera.

could be slaughtered for not ensuring that the gods had been worshipped properly.

So the concept of divine kingship was central to the rule of Egypt: the pharaoh was seen as an emissary of the gods and while religious rites were being correctly performed and the universal principle of *maat* – justice, order and truth – were being maintained, life would continue to run a smooth course. But if an imbalance was to occur, then the kingdom would disintegrate into chaos, which would prevail until a new, stronger and more divine king arrived to take control. In spite of his divinity, it was acceptable to overthrow a king, should he be perceived to have lost favour with the gods. Then, he would simply be replaced by a ruler who was more pleasing to the gods, who would guide Egypt back to the old days of plenty.

LEFT: The 'Great Seat' or sanctuary at Dendera.

OPPOSITE: Queen Nefertari's temple, also dedicated to the goddess Hathor, at Abu Simbel.

Chapter Six
BURIAL CUSTOMS &
SACRED ANIMALS

CHAPTER SIX
BURIAL CUSTOMS & SACRED ANIMALS

In Predynastic Egypt, up to around 3000 BC, the dead were simply laid in shallow holes, though some burial goods were also included, such as containers holding food, jewellery, and slate palettes. The provision of food was considered vital in securing the passage of the deceased to the Afterlife, while jewellery iwas an indication of status. The palettes were provided simply so that eye paints could be prepared.

Other objects placed in these shallow graves were directly connected with beliefs or rituals, rather than the practical considerations of the Afterlife. In tombs of the Naqada I period, a chronological phase in the Upper Egyptian Cultural Sequence of Predynastic Egypt, clay models of garlic were found, while wooden boards were used to line a tomb at Qau, which are believed to herald the appearance of the coffin.

By the Early Dynastic Period, up to around 2700 BC, wooden coffins were often used in important burials, placed in huge, mud-brick *mastabas*, while poorer Egyptians continued to be buried in shallow holes in the ground. For the most part, the dead were buried in bent-up positions, but by the second dynasty bodies were laid out full-length. In front of the corpse, a funerary meal was laid out, while other objects in the burial chamber included furniture, weapons, tools and even games.

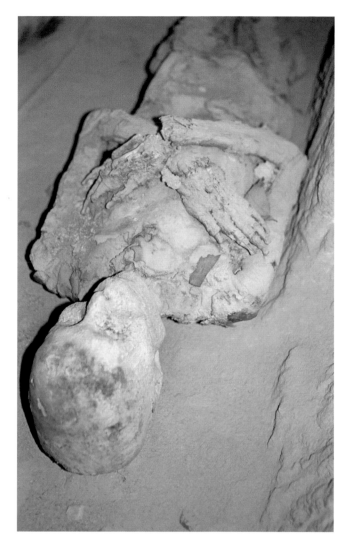

By the time of the Old Kingdom, burial practice seems to have shifted towards rock-cut or *mastaba* tombs, with wall reliefs decorating the offertory chapels and corridors of the tombs of the elite. These tended to show the dead being given food and other objects and, as a result, the objects themselves were not included in the tomb. A handful of goods were placed in the underground burial chamber, however, and some of these were of high quality, demonstrating the status of the deceased. Typical objects would have included sets of model copper tools, pottery, washing sets and jars. Ordinary people tended not to have coffins or jewellery, but in slightly richer burials some pottery and stone vessels were included, and a headrest would be placed beneath the head of the deceased.

Towards the end of the Old Kingdom, the focus shifted towards underground chambers. *Mastabas* were now less richly decorated, standard coffins had by now been introduced, and some of the chambers were decorated with lists of offerings.

OPPOSITE: Tombs at Jebel el-Mawta, the Mountain of the Dead, Siwa.

ABOVE: A mummy, found in sand in the tomb of Si-Ammon, a Greek merchant, Jebel el-Mawta.

RIGHT: Mural in the tomb of Menna, Valley of the Nobles, Luxor.

Coffins of the early Middle Kingdom had interiors painted with religious texts and pictures of objects, while small statues of the tomb-owner were placed in the vicinity. Other coffins had wooden models of craftsmen at work, and the heads of the deceased were often covered by a mask. Headrests were often provided, and sandals were left on the feet. Women were often buried with their jewellery, cosmetics and grinding stones, whereas men would be given weapons and objects showing their status in life. Pottery was now used to symbolize food, while flat drinking bowls and tall jars commonly appeared.

Another dramatic change occurred at the end of the Middle Kingdom period, running up to around 1550 BC. In court burials, the deceased was now shown as Osiris and sets of royal insignia were placed next to the body. Anthropoid (human body-shaped) coffins were by now becoming common, as were canopic jars, used for holding body parts. Coffins were now partly covered in gold, and jewellery was often left in the grave, along with miniature pottery vessels.

New arrivals began to appear in the form of *shabtis* – small inscribed adult figures, intended to perform heavy manual tasks for the deceased in the Afterlife. By the beginning of the 18th dynasty, only a single *shabti* would have been buried with the body, but later on a new one would be added for every day of the year. A further refinement was the addition of overseer *shabtis*,

LEFT: A pottery mummy, found in the Valley of the Nobles, Luxor.

OPPOSITE: A tomb in the Valley of the Nobles.

which supervised ten subordinate *shabtis*; consequently the burial sites of the elite could have as many as 36 overseer *shabtis* looking after 360 worker *shabtis*.

Huge numbers of *shabtis* were still being found in burial sites towards the end of the period, even though the overseer figures seem to have disappeared. Magical wands were now added, as were small limestone figures. Religious texts were written on various objects, including papyrus and pottery, and elaborate faience figures of animals, such as hippopotomuses, were also left in the grave.

During the 18th dynasty, rich burials could include a manuscript of the Book of the Dead, a set of around 200 magic formulae. These were, in effect, mortuary spells, divided into individual chapters. They were placed with the dead to help them make the transition through the Underworld towards a blissful Afterlife. Canopic jars were also included in these burials, as were anthropoid coffins.

Another change occurred during the late New Kingdom period. Now the objects placed in burials were specifically designed for the purpose, and heart-shaped scarabs, pectorals made of gold, amulets, *shabtis*, coffins and mummy boards, as well as the Book of the Dead, were often to be found. Poorer people would have had only a set of crude *shabtis* and their bodies would have been contained in coffins made of pottery.

LEFT: A royal sarcophagus from the Temple of Luxor.

OPPOSITE: The coffin of a priest in the Luxor museum.

By the 21st dynasty, officials were being buried in vast galleries and members of the royal families were laid in small tomb chambers. Burial equipment had begun to dwindle and *shabtis*, papyri and canopic jars had all but disappeared. By the late period, *shabtis* were back in use, and wooden figures of the gods were also included, as were amulets, canopic jars, the Book of the Dead, and elaborate coffins.

Enduring themes run through Egyptian death and burial customs. Foremost, must be the elaborate coffins and, of course, the practice of mummification. The coffin was an important item, and whether it was to take a royal body or that of a humbler person, its primary purpose was protection and preservation. Before coffins were used, Egyptians made do with mats, furs, baskets and pots.

The Egyptians believed being placed in a coffin allowed them to be reborn. In Ancient Egypt, a

OPPOSITE: The village of Gurna, near the Valley of the Kings, where villagers have been extensively rehoused in the name of archeology.

ABOVE: Wall painting of Anubis in Hatshepsut's Anubis chapel at Deir el-Bahri.

RIGHT: The goddess Hathor, depicted as a cow, and worshipped as a cow-deity from earliest times. Luxor museum.

PAGES 214–215: Processional route at Luxor.

OPPOSITE: Hathor as a cow, nursing Amenhotep. Chapel of Hathor, Deir el-Bahri.

LEFT: Modern statues of the cat-goddess Bastet, on sale in a Luxor bazaar.

ABOVE: Bastet, whose cult was centred at Bubastis.

sarcophagus (literally flesh-eater) was usually the external layer of protection for a royal mummy, with

OPPOSITE & ABOVE: King Taharqa, being protected by the god Amun in the form of a ram. From the temple at Kawa in Nubia.

ABOVE RIGHT: Avenue of ram-headed sphinxes at Karnak.

several layers of coffins, nested one inside the other.

The first early royal coffins were of stone, most of them very plain, with flat covers, while some had vaulted lids and were more elaborate. Early on, coffins and coffin walls were being painted with false doors, texts, pairs of eyes (to allow the deceased to see) and hieroglyphs. While coffin styles and decoration may have changed over time, anthropoid coffins first appeared in the Middle Kingdom, when they were first

used as interior containers for the body, before they were placed in rectangular outer coffins.

Coffins were nearly always oriented in a north-south position, while mention of Osiris would have been made on the outside eastern side of the coffin, with a burial scene, featuring Anubis, appearing on the opposite. By the 11th dynasty, text was in use inside the coffins and by the 12th dynasty, friezes of different objects were being applied to their eastern sides.

The anthropoid coffin provided a second image of the deceased, and lids were also decorated with vultures' wings. Later coffins were painted white, criss-crossed with bands representing mummy wrappings, and painted panels of the gods were incorporated with sacred text, some with gilded faces or golden bands. By the middle of the 18th dynasty, coffins used in non-royal burials were painted with black pitch.

By the time of the New Kingdom, wealthy Egyptians had multiple coffins, as well as sarcophagi, while lower-status individuals were still being buried in single coffins – mainly of pottery or reeds, but sometimes of wood. The middle classes were buried in nested coffins, made of various materials and with different shapes, the finest having been made of cedar. Gold and silver were always reserved for kings, though gold and silver gilding could be used to demonstrate an individual's relationship with the king.

By the late New Kingdom period, and particularly by the 20th dynasty, black resin coffins were being replaced by brightly painted representations of the gods on yellow backgrounds, and spells from the Book of the Dead were included, while in anthropoid coffins, the figure would be carved with forearms crossed on the breast. Women were shown with open hands, lying flat on their breasts, while men usually had clenched fists holding amulets.

PAGES 220–221: *Processional avenue with sphinxes, Karnak.*

RIGHT: *The goddess Mertseger, often depicted as a rearing cobra, was a protector of tombs.*

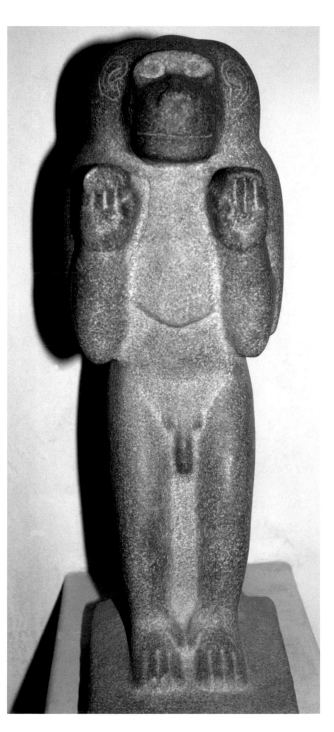

Mummies in coffins such as these were covered with a mummy board or false lid; this was in two pieces and echoed the shape of the lid. The upper part represented the face, collar and crossed arms, while the lower reproduced the mummy's bandages and there were seams between the bands. The new type of mummy board and lid became popular during the 19th dynasty because the deceased appeared as they did in life; the hands of the men were placed on their thighs and the women often held a decorative plant in their hands.

By the 21st dynasty, burials were no longer taking place in the Valley of the Kings or at Thebes. During the last decade of Ramesses XI's reign, new motifs began to appear on coffins, the emphasis being on Osiris and the worship of the sun. By the end of the 21st dynasty, the colour yellow had been superseded by red, white and light-blue, and coffins now had other motifs, particularly the Amduat, a funerary text documenting the sun god's journey through the 12 parts of the Underworld.

When Libyan rulers took control of Egypt during the Third Intermediate Period, new coffin shapes and styles became popular. There were still traditional cases that were deep enough to hold a mummy, but there were also shallower ones, their upper lids joining at the same level as the top of the mummy. There were also rectangular coffins, with vaulted roofs and four posts at the corners.

FAR LEFT: Babi, the dominant male baboon god, in the Nubian Museum, Aswan.

LEFT: A statue of the god Babi in the National Museum, Khartoum.

An effigy of Menhit, a lion-headed war goddess from Nubia, now in the Cairo museum.

Once the Nubians were in control of Egypt, very fine coffins were produced, some with foot pedestals, and others with scenes of judgement on their lids. Inside, there would have been excerpts from the Book of the Dead and scenes showing the Four Sons of Horus. By the 26th dynasty, coffins had a flat lower part, and a convex lid covered the mummy. Again, the Book of the Dead would have been in evidence, with excerpts written on the lid in vertical columns.

By the end of the period of independence, coffins and other mummy containers began to vary enormously: different regions began to prefer various styles and approaches, and foreign gods and the presence of the Greeks in Egypt began to take effect, showing their influence in many different ways.

Mummification is essentially a method of preservation, in which all moisture is removed from the body, leaving a dried-out husk that resists decay. In the hands of the Ancient Egyptians, mummification, by and large, was incredibly successful, and the facial features of bodies mummified 3,000 years ago, remain quite discernable to this day.

It is probable that this method of preserving the human body was discovered by chance. Although Egypt has little rainfall, it does have an abundance of dry sand and warm air, and bodies buried in shallow depressions in the sand would have dried out naturally over a period of time. By 2600 BC, or during the fourth and fifth dynasties, the Egyptians had begun to realize what was taking place, which led them on to ways of refining the process themselves. Mummification would continue well into the Roman period, and last for over 2,000 years.

As with so many other things in life, successful mummification depended on how much a family was prepared to pay. The best-preserved mummies are from the period of the New Kingdom, primarily the 18th to the 20th dynasties; because the bodies, including that of Tutankhamun, have been so well preserved, most of our knowledge of the subject comes from that time.

The process is believed to have taken around 70 days to complete, and was carried out by specially trained priests. Priests were already embalmers, with a wide knowledge of human anatomy, and were also able to carry out particular rituals and utter special prayers at specific times during the process.

The first task was to remove the internal organs, which were the quickest to putrefy. The brain was removed by inserting a hook through the nostrils and pulling out the brain tissue, then a cut was made in the left side of the abdomen through which the other organs were removed; the heart was left in place, since it symbolized all that had contributed to the deceased's individuality. Organs, such as the stomach, lungs and liver, were preserved separately, then placed in canopic jars that were buried with the mummy.

Later mummies would also have had their internal organs removed, which were preserved and replaced inside the body. The next major phase was to remove the remaining moisture from the body by covering it, inside and out, with natron, a mineral salt. Then the body would be left until most of the moisture had been absorbed. The embalmers then removed all the natron from the desiccated human form.

To make the body more presentable, sunken areas were filled with wads of linen and false eyes were added. The next process involved the wrappings, which required several hundred yards of linen. Slowly and carefully, the long strips were wrapped around the body, with fingers and toes sometimes wrapped individually, while amulets, prayers and magic texts were inserted between the wrappings.

After a certain amount of bandaging had taken place, resin would have been used to coat the bandages, before more wrapping were added. Once the final layers were in place, they were secured using thinner linen strips, and the mummification process was complete.

The pharaoh, or other wealthy individuals, would have probably begun their own tomb years or months before their death, which entailed inspecting it from time to time. Since it took 70 days to complete the process of mummification it was vital that the tomb be completed in time, with wall-paintings completed, statues added, furniture brought in, and all other symbolic items set in their correct place.

Priests were then able to perform the special funerary rites at the tomb, the most important being the Opening of the Mouth, which allowed the deceased to eat, speak and breathe during his journey to the Afterlife. The mummy was then put into the coffin, coffins or sarcophagus, placed in the burial chamber, and the entrance sealed.

The Egyptians believed the body to be the repository of an individual's soul or spirit, which was the reason why it was so important to preserve it. Though the body would remain in the tomb, the *ka*, or spiritual side of a person, together with the soul, would survive after death, and need all the offerings and objects that been left for it

in the tomb. The *ba* was the soul, which was free to leave the tomb, and the *akh* (the Shining One) was the part of the individual least bound to the earth, which would be required to take the journey through the Underworld, to final judgement, and hopefully, to the Afterlife.

Archeologists and medical specialists have been able to examine mummies for some time, using X-rays without destroying wrappings, and can speak with greater confidence regarding the process of mummification. Unwrapped bodies have also been subjected to autopsies, so it is possible to study the diseases of the time and the way that they were treated. It is also possible to estimate life-spans and average heights in Ancient Egypt, which, in turn has made it possible to estimate dates of royal accessions to the throne, while bloodlines can be determined by modern techniques.

Embalmers had an important part to play in Egyptian society. Most of their workshops, the *wbt* or places of purification, were outside the tomb enclosures, because certain dangers may have been attached to the mummification process. There were a number of different rites associated with mummification, but it is still unclear whether it was the complicated and extensive rituals themselves that led to the lengthy process, or whether it was the embalming itself that took up the time.

The embalmers, or priests involved in these rites, used a number of tools, particularly during the preparation of the body. A blade, usually made of obsidian and often referred to as 'the stone of Ethiopia', was used to make the incision in the abdomen to remove the internal organs. They also made use of everyday objects to provide support, and fingerstalls were used

to protect delicate areas. A scribe recorded the work and the embalmer would probably have worn a jackal-headed mask symbolizing Anubis, who was the god of death and embalming.

Embalmers had an intimate knowledge of the human body, and their profession was usually hereditary. They also supervised the construction of the coffin and the items that would be placed within the mummy wrappings or inside the tomb itself.

The unpleasant job of actually cutting into the body and removing the organs was left to people of low status, some of whom may have been convicted criminals. This was because the process was considered impure and precluded higher-caste individuals from carrying out the task.

Other specialists were also on hand: priests of Osiris performed the rituals, while others chanted and ensured that the ritual was being carried out correctly. It was the task of others to prepare the natron and the resin, but it was a priest's job to wrap up the body. In all, it was a complicated business that employed a great many people.

Human beings were not the only creatures to be mummified in Ancient Egypt. Various animal-worshipping cults had been in existence as far back as 4000 BC, and examples of ritual burials of animals were common in Predynastic times, with sites at Badari, Heliopolis, Maadi and Naqada revealing the mummified remains of dogs, cattle, monkeys and even gazelles.

OPPOSITE: Ammit, Devourer of the Souls of the Wicked, from the wooden bed tomb of Tutankhamun.

RIGHT: One of six sandstone lions from Basa, Sudan.

It is clear that Egyptians worshipped gods in animal form, one of the first possible examples being the divine cult of the sacred bull, established during the first dynasty. The Egyptians believed a powerful bull reflected the qualities and personality of the king: in other words, it symbolized his courage, strength, fighting spirit and virility. Bulls with specific markings were favoured by the priests, who looked out for black calves with white diamonds on their foreheads or shapes on their backs resembling eagles, while scarab markings under the tongue were thought to be yet another good sign. Once a suitable bull had been identified, it would be proclaimed a god and taken to the temple, where it would be respectfully treated.

The best known of the bull cults was that of Apis – a bull believed to be an incarnation of the god Ptah – and the birth of such a calf would have been an occasion of great celebration. The Festival of the Apis Bull was celebrated for seven days, and any child fortunate enough to smell its breath received the gift of predicting the future. The bull was sometimes asked to give advice on a specific matter, then offered food; it was considered a good omen if it ate the food, but bad if it refused. When the Apis bull died, and before it was buried, its internal organs were removed and it was embalmed. Then it was entombed in a crouching position, its head having been gilded or covered with a gold-leaf mask.

Probably one of the last of these cults continued until AD 362. This was the Buchis cult, in which the bull was believed to represent Re, Osiris and possibly the war-god Mentu. For generations, the cult had been in the habit of mummifying its bulls, then burying them in specially built tombs near Armant.

When the circumstances were favourable, therefore, animals could be manifestations of particular gods. The Egyptians believed the god took up residence in the animal and that the animal, in turn, assumed the attributes of the god. Depictions of Horus often show him as a falcon, so it was one step further to believe that an actual falcon was an embodiment of the god.

As far as the Ancient Egyptians were concerned, several criteria existed by which an animal would be judged sacred. Temple animals were kept in or near a temple, having been chosen because of their distinctive markings, where they would be venerated in much the same way as a cult statue, while other classes of sacred animal was kept in larger numbers, in the temple environs. The Egyptians did not believe a god was present in a single creature, but throughout the species. Hence all crocodiles and ibises were considered sacred.

At Saqqara, priests tended large flocks of ibises in a complex of buildings. The ibis was believed to be a manifestation of Thoth, who was sometimes shown as a man with the head of an ibis or as a full ibis. At Saqqara, large numbers of falcons sacred to Horus were also kept – though Horus is only one example of several falcon gods worshipped across Egypt. It follows, therefore, that many of these creatures would ultimately be mummified and buried, and in the case of the ibises, in a special necropolis of their own at Saqqara.

Lions were connected with the rising and setting sun, while the earth god, Aker, the god of today and tomorrow, was shown as a double sphinx – in other words, as two lions back to back – guarding the sun as it entered and departed the Underworld. Other gods were given the likeness of a lion or lioness, which

included Tefnut, Sekhmet, Hathor and Nefertem.

Lioness goddesses soon became cat goddesses, and the goddess Bastet eventually came to personify the domestic cat which, though it kept its sacred attributes, was also a practical animal, valuable for keeping grain stores free from rodents. In some cases, killing a cat was punishable by death, and some went to extremes of mourning, by shaving off their eyebrows when a pet cat died.

A necropolis for cats existed at Bubastis, a site sacred to the goddess Bastet, who is often depicted as a woman with the head of a cat. Bastet was a household goddess, but she was also seen as a protector of women, children and domestic cats, and was also associated with music, dance and fertility. Another side of the coin also existed in the person of the lion goddess Sekhmet – a war goddess associated with disease and pestilence. Together, the goddesses represented duality in nature and the way in which its forces were arranged throughout the universe.

Living in a country such as Egypt made it necessary to co-exist with dangerous creatures, such as scorpions, snakes and crocodiles. Because the Egyptians associated the animals with their gods, they were able to see them in a new light, leading them to revere and respect them, rather than regarding them as threats. It follows that the crocodile god, Sobek, depicted as a man with a crocodile's head, was imbued

OPPOSITE: The giant scarab or dung beetle at Karnak represents the god Khepri, the reborn sun at dawn.

PAGES 230–231: Statues of owls in the Temple of Ramesses II, Abu Simbel.

Monkeys and baboons had been associated from early times with the gods, some of whom were depicted as such. One of these was Hapy, one of the Four Sons of Horus, and Hapy himself was associated with mummification. Baboons also came to be connected with Thoth and Re, and green monkeys with Atum.

Baboons were kept at Memphis and in the temple of Ptah, but the ritual burial of such animals seems to have begun during the reign of Amenhotep III. It seems that at some point, mummifying monkeys became widespread, and several of them have been found in the ibis necropolis at Tuna el-Gebel, probably dating from the 26th dynasty. Later, mummified monkeys were interned in almost every animal necropolis, the largest numbers having been found at Saqqara, Abydos and in the Valley of the Monkeys near Thebes. Baboons were originally buried in simple wooden coffins, but from the 26th dynasty onwards they were usually mummified before being buried.

The ram was considered important to the Ancient Egyptians, both for its fertility and its warlike attributes. A particular ram, with long, wavy horns and a heavy build, was associated with the god Banebdjetet, who had a cult centre at Mendes dating from Predynastic times. He is regarded as the supreme arbitrator, who intervened to stop Horus and Set's battle to the death. Osiris later wore similar horns, when the mummified rams at Mendes came to be regarded as manifestations of Osiris-Re.

Relief from the Temple of Sobek and Haroeris, Kom Ombo.

Mummified rams were also found at Elephantine, when, in this particular instance, they were associated with the god Khnum or Khenmu, often depicted with the head of a ram. Another species with curved horns was adopted during the Middle Kingdom, and was closely associated with the god Amun, particularly during the 12th dynasty, when he was referred to as the Lord of the Two Horns. The processional route to the Temple of Amun at Luxor is flanked with ram-headed, lion-bodied sphinxes of this type.

Other gods were also given ram heads or ram horns, an example being the god Andjety, who was worshipped in the mid-Nile delta around the cult centre of Busiris, and was probably a forerunner of Osiris. Re is also sometimes seen as a ram-headed god, as is Harakhte (Harmakhet), the Horus of the dawn and the morning sun.

The cow was the personification of the goddess Hathor, and because the cow patiently gave of its nourishing milk to the Egyptian people, so too was Hathor regarded as a nurturer, linked also with conception and childbirth.

The goddess Heqet was often depicted as a frog-headed woman or as a frog itself, there being an association between frogs and fertility and ultimately resurrection. Egypt was overrun with these creatures when the Nile flooded, but the Egyptians knew the fertile soil that the Nile would leave behind would feed them forever. Other, older gods were also associated with the frog, such as Nun, Amun, Heh and Kek.

The goose was sacred to Geb, whose name means 'earth'. He was also known as the Great Cackler, and was subsequently depicted as a black goose, representing fertile soil. Isis, as the daughter of Geb, was sometimes described as the egg of the goose.

The hippopotamus occupied a special place in the mythology of Egypt. This was because Set, having murdered Osiris, was transformed into such a beast during his fight with Horus, Osiris's avenger. Though the male hippopotamus was seen as an evil beast, the female was believed to be a manifestation of Taweret, a goddess of fertility and childbirth. The pig is also associated with Set, who in the guise of a pig blinded Horus. It is probable that pigs were sacrificed to the moon once a year, in an event linking the blinding of Horus with solar and lunar eclipses. Set is also associated with the turtle, particularly because it is largely seen at night, thus making it symbolic of evil and darkness.

The ostrich represented Maat, the personification of justice, order and truthr. She usually appears as a seated woman wearing ostrich feathers.

The god Khepri, a solar god of resurrection, is associated with the dung beetle or scarab, which lays its eggs in dung. The young, when they emerge, are therefore seen as symbols of creation or resurrection, having been born out of dead matter. It was believed that Khepri pushed the sun across the sky each day, rather like a dung beetle pushes a ball of dung.

The vulture was sacred to Nekhbet, who was originally the patron of Upper Egypt during the Old Kingdom period, and it is also associated with Mut, the Great Mother Goddess of Egypt. The vulture, and particularly its talons, was believed to be closely linked with rulership, and thus offered its eternal protection to the pharaoh.

There were, of course, mythical creatures, such as the gryphon, which had the body of a cat and the head of a falcon. Equally as fabulous was the serpopard, with its cat's body, long neck and leopard's head. Double-headed bulls were also sometimes depicted, as was a hippopotamus with a crocodile's back and tail. These creatures represented supernatural powers, and the Egyptians may have believed they actually lived in the wild, either in the desert or in the area surrounding the valley of the Nile; they were the Egyptian equivalent of the Loch Ness monster and the abominable snowman.

It should be remembered that the Ancient Egyptians were extremely superstitious, and while hunters occasionally claimed to have seen such beasts, they were obviously much too intelligent ever to let themselves to be caught.

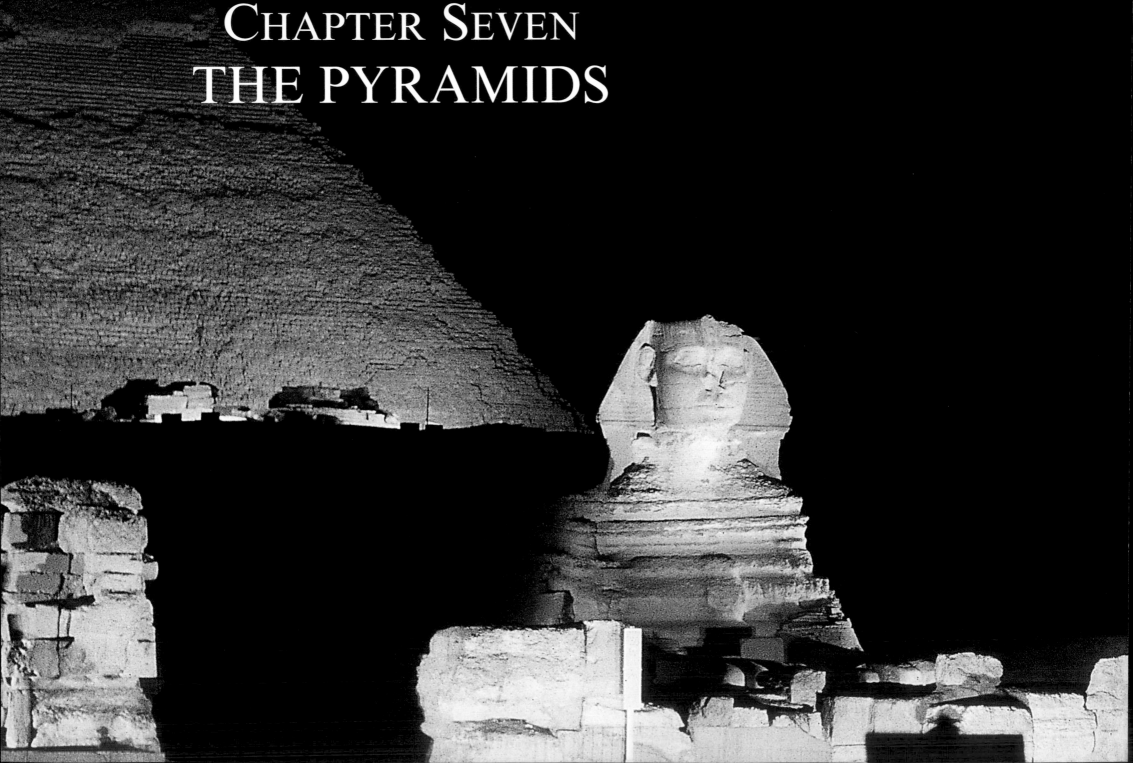

CHAPTER SEVEN
THE PYRAMIDS

Util the end of the Early Dynastic Period, Egyptian royalty and nobility were buried in tombs built from mud bricks, known as *mastabas*. These, in effect, were burial pits, surmounted by superstructures containing storerooms; these held the offerings that would be made to the dead.

At some point during the third dynasty, the pharaohs began to use stone, and the first tomb of this type, probably designed by the architect Imhotep, was planned for the Pharaoh Djoser. The ground selected was at Saqqara, overlooking Memphis, and the tomb was to be the first monumental step pyramid and the centrepiece of a large complex of stone buildings and courtyards. The first construction was far from simple, and numerous alterations became necessary. The pyramid was to consist of six steps, dressed with limestone, while beneath the pyramid itself, a deep shaft, giving access to corridors and rooms, was also planned. But some of these underground rooms were never completed, and it is possible that the original monument had only two chambers at the bottom of the shaft, despite the fact that several changes had to made, and no less than 11 shafts were sunk.

Compared with what had gone before, this step pyramid and its associated buildings, which included a mortuary temple, were of enormous size and complexity. We are not precisely sure what purpose the buildings surrounding the pyramid were meant to serve, or how they would figure in Djoser's Afterlife. But this was very much the prototype of a series of structures that would be embellished and amended over the coming generations. It still had elements of the old *mastaba*, having a tomb chamber, dressed with pink granite, and a simple entrance hole cut into the flat roof; but there were other rooms and chambers, as well as galleries with tiles and reliefs.

Another king, Sekhemkhet, of the third dynasty, also had a step pyramid built for him, which would originally have been around 230ft (70m) tall. This too was a complicated structure, in which various tunnels, corridors, doorways, arches and galleries were constructed underground, with a *mastaba* on the south side of the pyramid, constructed from stone blocks. This was simply a device to deceive grave robbers, which did not work, since they dug a tunnel to reach the tomb chamber and were successful in removing most of its contents.

Another pyramid, this time at Zawiyet el-Aryan, and possibly dating from either the second or third dynasty, was also discovered, classified as a layer pyramid rather than a step pyramid. It is possible the architect originally intended it to have six or seven layers, but it was never completed. The design of this pyramid differs from the other two, in that there may have been plans to add side galleries near the tomb chamber. It is probable that the pyramid was never occupied, because no sign of a sarcophagus or funerary equipment has been found.

There were also four small step pyramids at Seila, Zawiyet el-Mayitin, Naqada and El-Kula. Not much is known about them, however, but they may have been designed as four-step structures, possibly of mud covered with white plaster, because there was no limestone in the area.

The transition from a step pyramid to a true pyramid began during the fourth dynasty, and such a pyramid, though damaged, exists 30 miles (48km) to the south of Memphis at Maidum. This pyramid has an initial-stage *mastaba*, what is probably a small step pyramid, but it is a true pyramid from the outside. It seems that the original superstructure was intended as a seven-step pyramid, but it was then enlarged and what amounted to a coat of additional limestone added, providing a unique example of a step pyramid transformed into a true pyramid.

The Step Pyramid of the Pharaoh Djoser, Saqqara.

Nearly 30 miles to the north of this are two other pyramids, the most southerly of which was built by Seneferu, a pharaoh of the fourth dynasty. This has variously been called the Bent, Blunted or False Pyramid, and has all the appearance of having been completed at speed, the original plans having been scaled down at some point. The Bent Pyramid has two separate entrances, both of which slope down from the sides of the pyramid into the substructure. The entrance on the north face is nearly 40ft (12m) above ground level and extends over 241ft (73m) diagonally, down towards the subterranean rock. The body of the pharaoh was not found within the pyramid, and tomb robbers are presumed to have carried off both his body and his sarcophagus.

Close to the Bent Pyramid is the earliest tomb to have been completed as a true pyramid. It looks remarkably flat, as the pyramid sides are at an angle of only 43°. An entrance above ground level leads to three chambers, arranged in line, one behind the other. The first two are of identical size, but the third chamber, which is accessed by a short passage, has an elaborate roof. It is not clear who was buried in this pyramid, but it is generally believed to be the true resting place of Sneferu, making both pyramids attributable to him. Some think that because there were two pyramids, they were symbolic of Sneferu's control over both Upper and Lower Egypt.

OPPOSITE: Sneferu's Bent Pyramid at Dahshur.

ABOVE RIGHT: Another view of Djoser's Step Pyramid.

Khufu, Sneferu's son and successor, chose a plateau some 5 miles (8km) to the west of Giza, where he erected a pyramid of much greater size; two of his descendants would follow him, building pyramids on the same plateau, though slightly to the south. Taken together, the three are by far the most celebrated of the Egyptian pyramids.

The Greeks knew Khufu as Cheops and it is the pyramid of Khufu, also known as the Great Pyramid, that marks the apogee of pyramid-building in Egypt, its size and quality having made it a Wonder of the Ancient World. Over 2,300,000 blocks of stone would have been used in its construction, each with an average weight of 2.5 tons. The total weight would have been in

the region of 6,000,000 tons and the finished height was 482ft (146m). It is the largest and the oldest of the Pyramids of Giza. During Napoleon Bonaparte's campaigns in Egypt, he was told that there was enough stone in the three pyramids to build a wall a foot wide and 10ft (3m) high, that would contain the whole of France.

There has been much investigation into the structure of the Great Pyramid, most of which was carried out in the 19th century. From a distance, the pyramid appears largely intact, but it has suffered greatly in that parts of it have been removed for other purposes. Most of the outer facing of limestone has been stripped off and there is a large hole in the northern face, attributable to the Caliph Ma'mun, who in the 9th century believed the pyramid to be packed with treasure. Some of the stone was also removed to build bridges, canals, walls and houses in the area surrounding Giza and Cairo.

The entrance is on the north face, around 55ft (17m) above ground level. A passageway runs down from the entrance to the core of the pyramid and into the rock. After about 345ft (105m), the passage levels out before continuing horizontally for another 30ft (9m) before entering a chamber. On the west side of the passageway, near the entrance to the chamber, there is another recess, never completed, while there is yet another, opposite the entrance, that leads to a further blind passage.

The Great Sphinx, silhouetted against the Pyramid of Khufu at Giza. Shown opposite is the scene illuminated at night.

The entrance to the burial chamber itself can be found 60ft (18m) from the entrance. The mouth of the passageway was originally covered with a slab of limestone, but at some point must have collapsed. The corridor here ascends for 129ft (39m) and leads into a gallery 153ft long and 28ft high (47 x 8.5m). The Grand Gallery, as it is known, has walls of polished limestone, at the end of which is a narrow passage leading to the granite King's Chamber, where there were considerable defences against grave robbers.

There are four wide slots cut into the walls of the antechamber, three of which extend to the floor, the other into the roof of the passage. It is believed the slots were intended to take a portcullis, which could be lowered using ropes. There were also blocks of granite, resting one on the other, which would have filled the space right up to the ceiling; without these, grave robbers would have found it a simple matter to enter the King's Chamber.

Close to the west wall lies a rectangular, granite sarcophagus, which would once have contained the body of the king. The ceiling of this chamber alone is said to weigh in the region of 400 tons, the intention being that the weight and strength of the stone would have prevented the chamber from caving in.

It is probable that the pyramid was robbed towards the end of the Old Kingdom period, the thieves having

LEFT: A close-up showing the construction of Khufu's pyramid.

OPPOSITE: Painting on the inside of a pyramid wall, Giza.

forced their way through the entrance, though after that the entrance was possibly resealed.

Opposite the east face of the pyramid there was once a mortuary temple, connected to a causeway through a doorway. At right angles to the upper part of the causeway were three smaller pyramids, each with a small, ruined chapel. The first pyramid may have belonged to Khufu's favourite queen, the second was probably his daughter's, and the third belonged to his half-sister, Queen Henutsen. The causeway would originally have been a passageway made of polished stone, decorated with carved pictures of animals.

Another royal tomb was discovered close to the first of the small pyramids, the tomb lying at the bottom of a vertical shaft, some 99ft (30m) deep. Inside, an alabaster sarcophagus was found belonging to Queen Hetepheres, Khufu's mother and Sneferu's wife. The body had been removed, but the canopic chest containing the removed body parts was found intact. It is believed that robbers broke into her tomb soon after her burial, causing Khufu to remove her body and transfer it to another tomb at Dahshur or possibly elsewhere.

What is striking about the Great Pyramid is that it is not surrounded by the tombs of other relatives and officials, which suggests that Khufu had not intended it to be at the centre of a necropolis. To the south of the Great Pyramid is the Great Sphinx, which is 240ft long and has a height of 66ft (75 x 20m).

The second pyramid of the Giza plateau, that of Khafre (Chephren), is situated on slightly higher ground than the Great Pyramid, which gives the immediate illusion that it is taller. But when it was originally built, and the Great Pyramid was still intact,

it was about 10ft lower. It is also 48ft (15m) smaller in each direction than the Great Pyramid. At the apex of the pyramid, most of the original outer casing is intact, and some is still in place at the base. The stone, however, is different from that of the Great Pyramid, in that the upper part is of limestone and the lower of red granite, while the capstone, which has long since disappeared, was probably also made of granite.

The sides of the Pyramid of Khafre are steeper than those of the Great Pyramid and there are very few similarities inside. The pyramid has two entrances, both of which are on the north face, the first being some 50ft (15m) above ground level, the other having been cut into the rock foundations in the surrounding pavement. Both descend at roughly the same angle. The upper entrance has a low, narrow passageway, which passes through the core of the pyramid before levelling out when it reaches the rock beneath, then continues in a straight line until it reaches the tomb chamber. The passageway of the sloping section, and most of the one

that is horizontal, are lined with red granite, and where the granite lining ends, slots have been cut to hold a portcullis, its damaged remains being still in place. The tomb chamber is cut out of the rock, with a pointed, gable roof consisting of limestone slabs.

The lower passageway enters the ground at roughly the same angle as the upper passageway. After descending, it flattens out for a while before rising steeply, when it joins the upper corridor and continues on to the tomb chamber.

Buildings, consisting of rough limestone faced with dried mud, surround the pyramid, and would once have been the homes of the workers and masons.

The third pyramid of the Giza group stands towards the south-west corner of the plateau. It probably belonged to Menkaure (Mycerinus), who was a well-respected but little-known pharaoh. The Pyramid of Menkaure is only about a quarter of the size of the Great Pyramid, and stands a little over 200ft (60m) tall, though it was probably taller when it was built. The upper portion is faced with dressed limestone, but the lower is covered with red granite and, in some places, has never been properly finished. The intention was probably to cover the entire pyramid with granite, but the idea was abandoned.

ABOVE LEFT: Detail of a pyramid.

OPPOSITE: Pyramid of Khafre at Giza.

PAGE 248: The pyramid complex of Menkaure at Giza.

PAGE 249: The three pyramids of the Giza plateau.

OPPOSITE: Another view of the pyramids at Giza.

ABOVE: Pyramid tombs at Jebel Barkal, Sudan.

the antechamber and the burial chamber. Two additional chambers were added, the first, a rectangular room hollowed out of the rock and reached by a flight of steps. The second chamber is situated at the far end of the passageway, is dressed completely in granite, and has a pointed roof.

It was here that the body of Menkaure was originally discovered. However, the mummy was lost when the ship transporting it to England sank off the Spanish coast. A wooden coffin lid, now in the British Museum, was found bearing Menkaure's name, but bones found in the coffin were carbon-dated and were found to date only from early Christian times.

Three subsidiary pyramids lie close to Menkaure's pyramid, but none of them appears to have been completed. The largest is at the eastern end of the three and was partially dressed with granite, while the other two seem to have had work carried out on their inner cores before work was abandoned. In the second of the three pyramids, human bones, believed to have belonged to a young woman, possibly a queen or princess, were found inside a small granite sarcophagus. The largest of the pyramids could well have belonged to Menkaure's principal queen, Khamerernebty II, while the ownership of the last pyramid is unknown.

Djedefre, a fourth-dynasty pharaoh, who possibly ruled between Khufu and Khafre, may have been the owner of another pyramid, sited 5 miles (8km) to the north of the Giza plateau. Unfortunately, very little of it remains, apart from an open trench sloping down to the base of a vertical shaft that is about 30ft (9m) deep. This may have been an abortive attempt to create a pyramid, as it was clearly abandoned shortly after.

There are signs that changes were made to the internal parts of the pyramid: initially a tunnel was dug through the rock, leading to a rectangular burial chamber, but this design was changed and the floor of the chamber was lowered. A second passageway was cut beneath the first, to allow the true entrance to slope down into the body of the pyramid, the passageway having been lined with granite where it enters the rock. The passageway flattens out, then continues along into an enlarged antechamber, decorated with carved panel-like walls; there are three granite portcullises between

Also associated with Djedefre, because a plaque bearing his name was found on site, is the so-called Unfinished Pyramid at Zawiyet el-Aryan, excavated between 1904 and 1905. It consists of an open trench, with a sloping floor and a vertical shaft that has been roughly hewn, with red granite on the floor. At the lower end of the trench, a pit has been partially filled with limestone blocks. An oval granite sarcophagus was sunk into the floor.

What is incredible about pyramid-building during the fourth dynasty is the sheer scale of the projects; some of the blocks of local stone in Menkaure's mortuary temple weighed as much as 220 tons each, while 30-ton blocks of granite had been transported 500 miles (800km) from Aswan. While this was a massive undertaking, there were practical reasons why the blocks were so huge, in that fewer joints would have been necessary, making for improved stability.

It would also have been impossible, especially during Khufu's reign of around 23 years, to have completed such a vast project without talented masons on hand, who knew how to cut hard granite. Equally impressive are the numbers of statues found: it has been calculated that for Khafre's second pyramid complex alone, between 100 and 200 statues were made, and similar numbers would have been present both in the Pyramid of Menkaure and in the Great Pyramid. In fact, virtually every private tomb at Saqqara and Giza featured statues of their owners.

Jebel Barkal, in the Western Desert, once the royal necropolis of Tuthmose III's ancient city of Napata.

In addition to these, many of the temples and causeways related to the fourth-dynasty pyramids bear sculptured reliefs. Fragments of these have been found and hundreds of craftsmen must have been employed for generations to complete this work alone.

According to legend, the first three kings of the fifth dynasty were Userkaf, Sahure and Neferirkare, and they all built sun temples in honour of the god Re. There are references to six of these temples, but of primary importance is the sun temple built by Niuserre, and in particular his pyramid, which showed pyramid-building was back in fashion. It was constructed a mile to the north of Abusir, on the edge of the desert at Abu Gurab. However, the pyramids of this period were inferior to those of the past, and many were simply cores of small stones covered in a limestone casing. As a result, not many have remained, and what have survived are little more than heaps of rubble.

Limestone, both from the pyramids themselves and from the reliefs belonging to Sahure, Neferirkare and Niuserre, were unfortunately removed by local inhabitants for use elsewhere. Only 60sq ft (6m^2) of Sahure's complex, lying in fragments, still exists, and even less has survived belonging to Niuserre. Sahure's complex has a pair of landing stages, with ramps connected to them, that give access to the River Nile. As for the remaining example belonging to Neferirkare, it is likely that work was abandoned before many of the reliefs were completed.

Userkaf built his pyramid at Saqqara, with a mortuary temple to the east, very close to the north-east corner of the Step Pyramid of Djoser. Unfortunately, we can only guess at the magnificence of his pyramid complex: what is known, because its head

is in the Cairo museum, is that a colossal seated statue of the king, carved in red granite, probably faced the pyramid, while other cult statues of the king stood in niches in the temple walls.

Unfortunately, Sahure's pyramid at Abusir has suffered greatly, both internally and externally. When it was completed, its sides would have measured 257ft at the base and its vertical height would have been 162ft (78 x 49m), but most of the limestone casing has since disappeared. The passageway, which led down to the burial chamber and was choked with masonry that had fallen from the structure of the building, sloped downwards for around 14ft (4m), then proceeded horizontally for 27ft (8m). At the end was a granite portcullis and beyond that another slope, before the oblong burial chamber could be reached. The passageway was lined largely with limestone and with granite around the portcullis. The burial chamber itself was made of limestone blocks, and had a pointed roof, the largest of the blocks being 25ft long, 9ft wide and 12ft thick (8 x 3 x 4m), though only two of them were completely intact.

To the east of the valley temple was a portico with a black polished basalt floor and a limestone ceiling, the latter painted blue and decorated with golden stars. There seem to have been attempts to make the buildings as magnificent as possible: columns were carved to represent date palms, and reliefs in the hall probably showed the king as either a sphinx or a gryphon, trampling his enemies. The pharaoh is shown in the act of killing a Libyan chief and inscriptions indicate that hundreds of thousands of cattle, asses, deer and sheep were taken as booty and brought back to Egypt from Libya.

Neferirkare probably ruled for around ten years, his pyramid complex being very like Sahure's, but much bigger. He undoubtedly died before it was completed, and in all probability when only the foundations had been laid. The causeway was probably completed, and statue niches and the sanctuary of the inner temple were under way. The pyramid is unfinished, and compared with that of Sahure is 360sq ft (33m²) at the base, and would have had a height of 228ft (69m), which makes it slightly bigger than the Pyramid of Menkaure. Very little remains of the outer casing, the lower part of which is made of granite.

Neferefre, who was Neferirkare's successor, began to build a pyramid a little to the south-east. Niuserre continued the construction of the pyramid and the mortuary temple, but chose to complete it with wooden columns standing on limestone bases. Niuserre's own complex is slightly different from that of Sahure, and red granite, limestone and black polished basalt were used in various combinations to construct the valley building. The sanctuary is due east of the burial chamber, and south-east of the main pyramid lies a subsidiary pyramid.

Djedkare Isesi was a successor to Niuserre and built his pyramid to the west of Saqqara. It is known by its Arabic name, which translates as the Pyramid of the Sentinel.

The final pharaoh of the dynasty, Unas, decided to build his pyramid to the south-west of the Step Pyramid enclosure, and its causeway is probably the best preserved of all. It is some 750yds (690m) long and some of the blocks used to bridge in the embankments were taken from the Step Pyramid enclosure, which leads us to think that Djoser's

pyramid was falling apart at this time. Along the passageways, and in the mortuary temple, are well-preserved low-relief scenes, carved into the stonework; these show servants, animals and craftsmen, and were originally painted in bright colours. The ceiling was given a sky-blue background and golden stars were painted on top.

In modern times, the archeological excavation of the mortuary temple began in 1900 and continued for around 30 years, when the layout of the passageways, the inner temple, the reliefs, and the types of paving used, were all revealed.

The pyramid itself was probably around 62ft (19m) tall, which is comparatively small compared with a pyramid of the fourth dynasty. The entrance is on the north side, not through the face of the pyramid but through the pavement. Three portcullises of granite block the passageway and once negotiated, lead to a long, narrow room in the east wall, where there are three statue niches. The burial chamber is to the west, and there was a stone sarcophagus at the far end, which was found to be undamaged. This had been robbed of its contents long before the 1880s, when the first archeologist gained access to the pyramid itself. All the rooms were constructed from limestone, with the exception of the area around the sarcophagus, which was of alabaster.

The walls of the vestibule and burial chamber are covered in hieroglyphic inscriptions, known as the Pyramid Texts, and these would also be found in the pyramids of sixth-dynasty pharaohs, including Teti. They did not tell a story as such, but were a collection of magic spells or formulae, many of which occur in other pyramids, though very few are repeated. Unas's

pyramid contains 228 spells out of a known total of over 700.

The Pyramid Texts were designed to ensure a happy Afterlife for the pharaoh, and the act of writing down the words was sufficiently powerful for the desires of the pharaoh to be realized. The presence of the spells, together with other provisions, ensured the pharaoh would want for nothing in terms of food and drink, and that he would be protected by the written word in the event of the priests failing to carry out their duties.

The Pyramid Texts actually predated the fifth and sixth dynasties. Some of them clearly refer to much earlier periods and make references to *mastabas*. It is clear the priests used old funerary spells, updated some of them, and added new ones of their own. Being written in hieroglyphs, they possessed a special magic power; in order to protect the pharaoh from, say, scorpions, for example, the scorpions were depicted minus their stings.

By the Middle Kingdom, however, there was a change: now the Pyramid Texts were written on the inside of rectangular wooden coffins, rather than on the walls, and were now known as the Coffin Texts.

Pyramids continued to be built by later pharaohs, but none was as magnificent as the vast Great Pyramid and its companions. But how were pyramids constructed and why were they built? The answer lies far beyond the desire to protect the mummified body of a dead ruler.

Valley of the Queens, Luxor.

The first job for the constructors, once a suitable site had been found, was to remove layers of sand and gravel, so that the pyramid could rest on a foundation of rock. The rock would then need to be levelled and smoothed, with pieces either removed or used to fill up depressions. This was done so skilfully that the area around the Great Pyramid, for example, only deviates by half an inch.

As near as possible, the base of the pyramid needed to form a perfect square, and its exact orientation had to be calculated. This was no easy task, seeing that there were no compasses, and could only be done by observing the stars and planets. The rising and the setting of the sun indicated east and west, but the fact that many of the pyramids ended slightly off-centre meant that errors were still possible.

Two devices were used, the first being the *merkhet*, which consisted of a narrow, horizontal bar with a small block at the end. A hole was bored through the block and it was probably used as a shadow clock. The other device was known as a *bay*, and was a straight palm rib with a V-shaped slot cut into the widest end; this was probably used for surveying.

While the site was being prepared, the foundations of the causeway were being laid and limestone blocks for the outer casing of the building were being quarried. The limestone was sometimes extracted with the help of copper tools, including saws and chisels, but wedges and chisels were more often used. The chisel would be used to cut the block away from the rock and the wedge for detaching the blocks at their base.

Tombs in the Vally of the Nobles, west bank, Luxor.

Granite was a slightly more difficult proposition. Some of it was probably obtained from large boulders lying about the surface, but it still needed to be shaped. This may have been done by working wedges into the rock to split off slabs, while rubbing an abrasive powder onto the surface; alternatively, a metal tool was probably used to create the original slots for the wedges, which was a long and laborious task. Then the workforce had the problem of transporting the blocks from the quarry to the pyramid site.

The outer casing blocks of the Great Pyramid weighed around 2.5 tons each, the granite roof slabs in the king's chamber being a staggering 50 tons; some of the larger blocks, however, could weigh as much as 200 tons. Even when the blocks arrived at the pyramid site it would have been necessary to manhandle them into position – often well above ground level. Sledges were probably used to bring the blocks to the site and then moved by levers onto ramps. Wooden rollers would then have been used, but sheer brute force was required to slot the blocks into their precise positions. It is probable the Egyptians did not know about pulleys, so that when the original step pyramids were built, their lower levels would have been used as ramps to raise the blocks to the higher parts of the pyramid.

The core of the pyramid was made of local stone, the bottom surface of the blocks being smooth, while their sides and top were left rough, to help them knit together. Gaps would often be left unfilled, but care would have been taken to ensure that each new course of stone still formed a square, getting smaller and smaller until the top of the pyramid was reached. Once completed, the outer limestone casing was then added: this was a much more delicate job, because the joints

needed to be precise and any irregularities had to be ironed out to prevent the clean lines of the finished pyramid from being spoiled.

Masons then dressed each of the stones, the work obviously beginning at the bottom, with each new course fitted to the course below. Once the top had been reached, a capstone of granite was placed at the apex of the pyramid.

During all of this, particular attention would have been paid to the passageways and chambers within the pyramid. Work would have been completed on the interior before the surrounding courses of core masonry had risen to a height that would form the roof of the corridors and chambers. It is clear that the roofing slabs of the king's chamber in the Great Pyramid had been fitted together outside the pyramid, then numbered and put into their final positions within the pyramid. The sarcophagus itself, the portcullises and other features, would also have been installed before the rest of the pyramid had been completed.

Egyptologists are undecided as to whether or not the pyramids were ever painted. Traces of chemical elements unrelated to the stone have been found, and it may be that a type of plaster covered the dressed stone, which was then painted using a red ochre pigment.

Taking the Great Pyramid as an example once again, such was its size that some 400,000 men would have worked on it each year, divided into four groups of 100,000, each group working for three months. Given that the pyramid needed 2.3 million separate stone blocks, and that the average number of blocks transported annually was 115,000, the indication was that the construction took 20 years, taking the fact into account that work would not have been possible from

the end of July to the end of October, due to the Nile flood season.

It is believed that the pyramids, in the manner of their predecessors, the step pyramids, represented a staircase to heaven, by which the dead pharaoh could ascend to heaven when he wished or return to his tomb to enjoy the offerings left for him by his relations and the priests.

The Egyptians were not the only ancients in the Middle East to believe that heaven and the gods could be reached from a tall building, an example being the high brick towers of Mesopotamia, known as ziggurats, which were probably the inspiration for the Biblical Tower of Babel.

The history of the pyramids extends over 1,000 years and they were believed to bestow immortality. There have been other suggestions over the years as to their purpose: some believe they were repositories of wisdom and scientific knowledge, while others regarded them as places where corn was stored. What is true is that they were designed to be permanent monuments to the pharaohs, providing them with the means by which they would be ultimately united with the gods.

LEFT: A depiction of Osiris on a pillar in the tomb of Nefertari, Abu Simbel.

OPPOSITE: The Valley of the Kings, Luxor.

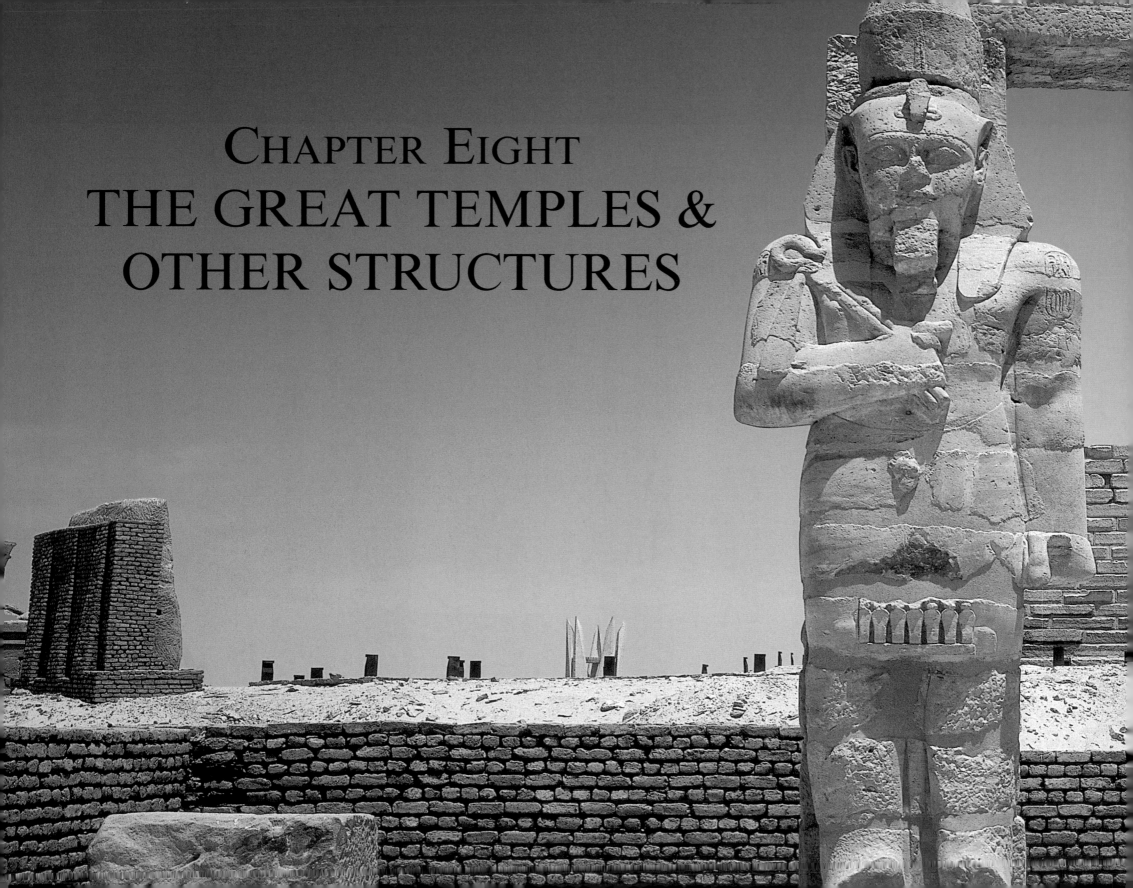

Chapter Eight
THE GREAT TEMPLES &
OTHER STRUCTURES

CHAPTER EIGHT
THE GREAT TEMPLES &
OTHER STRUCTURES

When applied to the Ancient Egyptians, the term temple can be misleading, since it covers a wide variety of structures used for many different purposes over a considerable period of time. Many of the large and ancient buildings of the Egyptians could be classed as temples in a religious sense, but they could just as easily have been fortresses, royal retreats, or centres of administration.

Mortuary temples were a part of the pyramid complexes of the early kings, perhaps the most famous being the temple at Karnak, which is the world's largest religious structure. It may not have been Egypt's largest temple, however, and the Temple of Ptah at Memphis may have been even larger; it was certainly older, and it was also used as the administrative centre of Egypt.

Egyptologists often prefer to use the term 'mansions of the gods' to describe temples, and sites at Dendera, Karnak and Kom Ombo could be termed as such, in that they were the abodes of the gods and existed to serve their symbolic needs. They were not

RIGHT: Hathor-headed capitals in the hypostyle hall at Dendera.

OPPOSITE: Relief from the tomb of Nefertari.

places of general worship, but places where the cosmic energy, *neter* (or specific aspect of a god) had chosen to dwell, bestowing its radiance on Egypt and its people. It was important that all activities within the temples were performed according to the laws of *maat*, otherwise the gods would abandon them and Egypt would descend into chaos.

Mortuary temples served a similar purpose, because the pharaohs were considered to be gods in their own right; consequently they were given the same attention accorded to the older gods, and this included a mansion of their own after they had died. Mortuary temples, tended by the pharaohs' cult followers, also served to keep the pharaoh-gods uppermost in the minds of their people.

Some served a dual purpose: for example, Queen Nefertari's temple at Abu Simbel was dedicated to the goddess Hathor as well as to the queen herself. A larger temple was built alongside for Nefertari's husband, Ramesses II, and even this had another purpose, its sheer monumentality making it a potent reminder of Egypt's domination of her southern neighbours.

Many temples belonging to the various dynasties are scattered around Egypt, but those that have been able to survive the ravages of time, and are the most complete, can be found in the south. These include some dedicated to a major god, others associated with several gods. The valley temples were believed to be imbued with the *ka* of a departed king. Their monumental gateways connected with the king's mortuary chapel, and other, more specialized temples, would have been set aside for coronations, sun worship, for festivals, and as repositories for statues.

Over time, many of the temples, Luxor and Karnak, for example, became parts of larger complexes, because individual pharaohs liked to add to them during their reigns, and even though the temples varied in their architecture and purpose, most of them had features in common. Mortuary temples built for the fifth-dynasty pharaohs nearly always had an outer area, consisting of an entrance corridor and an open courtyard leading to an inner sanctuary, while minor

chambers and buildings were added to the outer section, including places where temple guards were posted. Between the outer section and the sanctuary there would usually be a corridor and a doorway leading into the sanctuary. This consisted of a dark chapel, where the figure of the *neter* was enshrined; there would have been an offering hall with an altar beside the chapel, and there could even be additional rooms within the sanctuary itself.

Over time, therefore, an Egyptian temple could become an extremely complex structure, with an approach and entrance flanked by pylons or vast columns, an inner enclosure, and with an inner sanctuary at its heart. The external area was usually open to all, but in most cases the inner sanctum could be accessed only by priests, while in other cases only high-ranking priests or the pharaoh himself were permitted to enter. Surrounding the temple were sacred lakes, storage areas, gardens, offices, libraries and schools.

The Egyptians relied on the Nile for their very existence, but it was also a means of transportation. Many of the temples, therefore, had large docking areas that could accommodate boats, which carried the pharaoh, his relatives and entourage. The landing stages themselves were usually sited on canals running off the River Nile, which allowed items, as well as people, to be easily loaded and unloaded. This was particularly useful when transporting materials required for the many building projects. The landing stages were also areas where high-ranking visitors would be greeted, and cult statues were often placed there to be used in processions and ceremonials.

Statues usually marked the path from the landing stage to the temple itself, and could be representations either of the gods or the king, while following the New

ABOVE LEFT: A ba spirit (left) in the tomb of Nefertari.

OPPOSITE: The Temple of Nefertari, Abu Simbel.

Kingdom period, protective sphinxes, such as the ram-headed sphinxes that lined the route to the temple of Amun at Karnak, would also be used.

Way stations, built as simple resting places, also lined the route, some of them designed to house ceremonial boats. The temple itself was surrounded by a stout wall, providing spiritual as well as physical protection from evil or attack, and making the temple easier to defend; it also provided a symbolic boundary, separating the realm of the gods from the ordinary world – the sacred from the profane.

Sometimes, enclosing walls were constructed using alternating convex and concave sections. This had both a symbolic as well as a practical purpose: the wave pattern replicated the waters of the Nile, and at the same time helped to prevent the walls from swelling and cracking. Invariably, the walls were built of mud brick, and could be as much as 30ft (9m) thick; some of these walls had rounded battlements, while others had fortified gateways.

Obelisks, symbolic of the sun god Re, and a pyramid in another form, became common during the New Kingdom period and were usually erected in pairs outside the enclosure wall, their purpose being to commemorate important events. Unfortunately, only a handful of standing obelisks remain in Egypt, many of them having been removed and taken abroad.

Even larger than the obelisks, which could be taller than the temple itself, were the colossal statues, usually of the pharaohs, cut from vast blocks of limestone, sandstone or granite. They were made deliberately large to reflect the power of the king and place him on an even footing with the gods, the idea being that the

ordinary people could look up at the enormous statue and be filled with awe. The largest of these are the Colossi of Memnon and the Colossi of Ramesses II, at Luxor, which are some of the largest objects ever to have been constructed from a single block of stone. In his time, Ramesses II probably commissioned more such works than any other pharaoh.

Pylons were used either to create a grand entrance to a temple or to be enclosed within the temple itself. These were massive structures, usually filled with rubble cleared from the building site. Two pylons were used either side of the entrance, which would be about

OPPOSITE: The Temple of Nefertari, dedicated to Hathor, at Abu Simbel.

LEFT: Queen Nefertari, the Great Royal Wife of Ramesses the Great, offering a sistrum and a flower to Anqet the Embracer, goddess of fertility. The Great Temple of Re-Harakhte, Abu Simbel.

PAGE 268: Aeriel views of the temples of Re-Harakhte and Nefertari-Hathor.

PAGE 269: Interior of the temple of Nefertari-Hathor.

PAGES 270–271: Abu Simbel, site of the temples of Re-Harakhte and Nefertari-Hathor.

PAGE 272: The mortuary temple of Seti I at Abydos.

PAGE 273: Temple of Tuthmose III, with its sacred lake, Karnak.

squatting or kneeling before the deity. The Egyptians believed the soul lived on inside a statue after a person's death, and positioning their own statue in this holy place ensured their soul remained close to the god.

Because the temple priests never refused a statue, the outer courtyards usually became cluttered with statuary over the generations, though the older statues would have been removed from time to time and buried beneath the temple courtyard. A cache of some 900 stone statuettes, dating from the 20th dynasty through to the Greek period, have been found at Karnak.

The outer courtyard was as far as the ordinary Egyptian was allowed to go, the area beyond this point being the preserve of purified priests. Directly beyond this courtyard lay what was known as a hypostyle, a pillared hall surrounded by smaller chambers. This was not the most sacred part of the temple, but its sheer enormity was impressive, with some hypostyles having as many as 100 pillars. In larger temples, these halls were sometimes repeated, gradually becoming more elegant as they approached the most sacred areas of the temple. By the time of the 19th dynasty, for example, around three hypostyle halls would have been added to the first, and particular ceremonies would have been carried out in each.

The enormous number of pillars effectively prevented people from prying into the building, though the hall was usually bisected by a processional route,

ABOVE LEFT: Depiction of the god Horus in the mortuary temple of Rameses III, Medinet Habu, Luxor.

OPPOSITE: Queen Hatshepsut's mortuary temple at Deir el-Bahri, Luxor.

half the height of the pylons; the pylons could also be decorated with reliefs, and sometimes had long poles attached to them from which banners were hung.

Having passed the pylons, in some of the larger temples, the visitor would enter a courtyard, only to see even more pylons ahead, as well as further courtyards. The courtyard itself acted as a kind of buffer zone, separating the outside world from the sanctified parts of the temple, and was usually rectangular, with colonnades along its sides. Courtyards were nearly always paved, with an altar from which offerings were

made; in some of the earlier temples, there were porticoes on raised platforms. The outer courtyard was the place that the common man could enter to celebrate a special occasion. There would have been hieroglyphs on the walls, representing the people of Egypt, and the pharaoh would be shown carrying out military operations, religious rites, presiding over a festival or worshipping the gods.

Around these outer courtyard areas, statues were ranged, some of them of the kings and gods, while others would have been of lesser mortals, either

passing through the central axis of the building, when the pillars became separated. Because the windows were set high in the walls and the doorways were barely visible, very little light was admitted to the interior.

As was so often the case in Ancient Egypt, the hypostyle had both symbolic and practical purposes. Although pillars were needed to support the sandstone architraves and roofing slabs, the structure also reflected certain Egyptian myths that the sky was supported above the earth on columns. The temple at Karnak is a good illustration of this, having columns designed to look like papyrus or lotus stems, and with column capitals resembling buds or marshland plants. The temple at Karnak has no less than 134 columns, some of which are nearly 80ft (24m) tall. It bears some resemblance to a Roman basilica, but, of course, is very much larger.

Doorways were of great importance, the doors themselves being usually made of wood, covered with metal, while others were cast entirely from metal. Wooden doors were commonly given a copper covering or could be plated with bronze, electrum or gold. They were mounted on wooden pivots, set into sockets in the floor and the lintels of the doorways. In some temple complexes each of the doors had their own names and were decorated with inscriptions and texts. Some doorways also bore images of the pharaoh, so that anyone entering the inner temple was symbolically cleansed. The doors had other symbolic purposes, in that they were seen as thresholds to other worlds, and

the ritual act of opening them was likened to the opening of the door to heaven.

Some of the temples were given false doors, intended not to confuse robbers, but to provide a route whereby the gods could leave heaven and enter the human world. Many inner sanctuaries also had false doors, usually located to the back, through which the god was able to gain access to his own sanctuary.

Statues had a particular role to play within the temple itself. The statue of a god was regarded as the embodiment of that god and, as such, was treated accordingly. It was fed, clothed and washed and even taken to visit other temples, where chambers were set aside for the statue and its priests; there would also have been places where the priests could prepare themselves for ceremonies, which accommodated clothing, incense and other important items to be used in rituals.

Crypts and hidden chambers were often built beneath the floors or into the walls, some of which have as yet unknown symbolic purposes, while others were used to hide the temple's treasures out of sight, or be used by priests when meditating.

The roof was also used for rituals, particularly in temples connected with sun gods. Here there were drainage systems with gargoyle spouts, which allowed the rainwater to run off the roof. It was the custom for a statue of the falcon god, Horus, to be carried in a portable shrine onto the rooftop at Edfu, where he would wait for the sun to rise.

ABOVE: Detail from Hatshepsut's mortuary temple.

OPPOSITE: Overview of Ramesses III's mortuary temple at Medinet Habu.

PAGES 278–279: Court of Amenhotep III, Luxor.

Beyond the actual hypostyle hall was the sanctuary itself, which usually consisted of a number of other chambers and halls. One of the most important was the offering hall, which would have had one or even several altars. It was here that sacrifices were made to the gods. In some cases the altar itself was placed in the inner sanctuary, while others would have been placed in the courtyard. The vast majority of altars were flat-topped blocks, like tables, while larger altars sometimes had steps leading up. Any decoration invariably showed the king bowing or kneeling before the god, with the king making an offering and the god providing the king with a gift in return.

Some temples would also have had barque shrines, housing a portable boat on which the statue of the god rested on ceremonial occasions. Some barques were purely symbolic and did not actually resemble boats at all, while the walls of the chapel were adorned with scenes of the king being transported in his barque. If there was no barque chapel, a canopy would be erected in the inner sanctuary to take its place.

LEFT: The mortuary temple of Mentuhotep II, Deir el-Bahri, Luxor.

OPPOSITE: The mortuary temple of Ramesses III, Medinet Habu.

PAGE 282: Ramesses III's temple: the Syrian gate.

PAGE 283: The façade of Ramesses III's temple at Medinet Habu.

The inner sanctuary was the holiest part of the temple, being most closely associated with the idea of the temple as the god's home. Typically they were deep, narrow rooms, situated towards the rear of the temple. Usually built on the main axis of the temple, there could be several inner sanctuaries in a temple, allowing the worship of different gods to be accommodated. For the most part, the shrine was accessible only to purified high priests and to the pharaoh himself, and if anyone else had the temerity to enter, the sanctuary was seen as desecrated, making it necessary that a new ceremony of dedication be performed.

Inside the sanctuary was the god's statue, usually housed in a shrine. In smaller temples the shrine was made of gilded wood, while in larger ones it was made of stone and had either gold-plated wooden doors or doors of solid bronze. The most common form of shrine had double doors that opened towards the temple entrance, and were occasionally mounted on a block of stone, accessed by several steps.

The size of the god's statue varied enormously, some being rather small, while others were vast. The larger statues tended to be made of stone or wood and for the most part were covered in silver, or in the case of sun gods, gold. Smaller statues could be made entirely of gold, with semi-precious stones for eyes and lapis lazuli for hair.

Those that were not mortuary temples could also have another room, known as the Chapel of the Hearing Ear. This allowed unpurified, ordinary Egyptians a degree of access to the god of the temple, though in actual fact, the chapel was usually just within the outer wall of the temple. The chapel could have a statue of the god, or merely a pair of his carved ears,

while a priest would sit in a hidden chamber, hearing petitions and replying to them on behalf of the god. Tuthmose III built the oldest surviving example of this type during the New Kingdom period, which, in this case, had a pair of alabaster statues, one of the pharaoh and one of the god Amun. Sometimes the chapel would be entirely detached from the temple complex, such as the small Temple of the Hearing Ear at Luxor, built by Ramesses II.

Temples had to be able to survive and to some extent be self-sufficient, which is why they were surrounded by services and facilities: unfortunately, many of these buildings were nowhere near as grand as the temple itself, and being made of mud brick have virtually disappeared. A number of key structures can be identified, however, including the *mammisi*, sacred lakes, nilometers, sanatoria, houses of life, storage facilities and living quarters.

The *mammisi* or birth house was usually located within the temple complex, at right angles to the main temple, its purpose being to celebrate the mystery of the divine birth. They probably date from the late Egyptian period, with examples from the 18th dynasty. However, the best-known *mammisi* is located at the Temple of Hathor at Dendera, dedicated to Ihy, the son of Hathor and Horus. The temple has a stone gateway rather than pylons at the entrance, which was built for the emperors Domitian and Trajan towards the end of the first century AD.

These buildings would have been decorated with text and pictures showing the courtship of the god's parents, and the god's birth and presentation. Also included would have been depictions of other gods, associated with him, in the act of praising the young god.

Sacred lakes were usually rectangular, with straight or slightly curved sides, though the sacred precinct of Mut at Karnak is actually horseshoe-shaped and another, known as the Osireion at Abydos, surrounds the shrine. On the side of the lake, facing the temple, would have been a stairway allowing access to the lake, regardless of the water level. The lakes were generally deeply-cut and lined with stone, so that groundwater could be utilized to advantage. The Egyptians called

LEFT: Another view of Ramesses III's mortuary temple.

OPPOSITE: Restoration in progress at Hatshepsut's mortuary temple at Deir el-Bahri, Luxor.

PAGES 286–287: The hypostyle hall in the Ramesseum at Luxor.

the lakes *shi-netjer* and they had both practical and symbolic purposes; they provided water for dawn bathing and purification ceremonies and offerings, while representing the primeval waters from which life originally came. Each morning, when the sun rose above the sacred lake, the life force was reborn.

One of the largest of the sacred lakes is at the temple of Karnak, and it is a good example of how such a lake would originally have looked. Geese were kept in pens close to the lake and would have been released each morning. The goose represented Geb, while temples associated with the god Sobek would have had crocodiles swimming in their sacred lakes.

Because their lives depended on the Nile, the Egyptians needed to know when the floodwaters would arrive, and they did this by means of a nileometer, examples of which can be seen at Aswan, Memphis and at the Nile's second and fourth cataracts in what was once Nubia. Nileometers were a means by which the height of the river could be estimated and recorded, and usually took the form of measuring steps situated at the water's edge. Some only had a few steps, while the nileometer on Elephantine island, at Aswan, for example, had 90, and was built during the Roman occupation of Egypt. On the island of Philae, near Aswan, there were two nileometers, one close to the temple of Nectanebo I, the other, further north, close to a Greek structure. (Philae island is now submerged and the Philae temple was taken apart and reassembled on Agilika Island, close by.) Nileometers may also have been regarded as gauges of a god's favour, since there are places where several were set close together, where only one would have been necessary: this is only a supposition, however.

Temples attracted many pilgrims, who came in order to be cured of sickness or injury, and where they would have sought healing from the gods and treatment from the priests and scholars. Very few of these sanatoria still exist, but ruins close to several temples could well have been used for the purpose, one of which is at Hatshepsut's temple at Thebes (Luxor), while there is another, much later one, at Dendera.

Particular temples were famous for treating certain conditions. At the temple dedicated to Hathor at Dendera are what remain of chambers where the sick were allowed to sleep, until messages from the gods came to them in dreams that helped them to recover. These were built round a central courtyard, in the centre of which, priests poured water over statues of the gods. The statues themselves were inscribed with magical texts, the idea being that the water would take up some of the magic, which in turn would be drunk by the sick who would be cured. Sometimes the sick were required to bathe in the water.

Closely associated with these sanatoria were medical centres, which the Egyptians knew as *per ankh*, literally 'houses of life'. These were repositories of religious and magical texts associated with the cults of the gods, and information was written, collated, copied

OPPOSITE: Column detail, the Temple of Khnum, Esna.

LEFT: Hypostyle hall, Karnak.

PAGE 290: Kiosk of Qertassi, Kalabsha, Aswan.

PAGE 291: Mortuary temple of Seti I, Luxor.

and edited before being placed in the *per medjat* or 'house of books'. Many of the texts mentioned the soul and how it could be healed.

Scholars also came to study medicine, and there were houses of life at Thebes, Esna, Edfu, Koptos, Abydos, Memphis and Akhmim, though it is not clear how many of them interacted with the temple itself.

At some point, probably in the New Kingdom period, copies of the Book of the Dead were also being produced. This was a collection of magic spells that could be used in the Afterlife, together with hymns of praise to various gods.

Another function associated with the house of life was to deal with correspondence, contracts, temple accounts and temple records. Ramesses IV, for example, made extensive use of the facility, claiming he had studied every single text in his quest to understand the secrets of the gods.

Although this was a place where religious texts were copied and read, other subjects were also studied, including art, astronomy, law, mathematics, magic, theology and rituals. There were no classrooms as such, but individuals could receive instruction from specialists in their field, provided they were rich enough to pay for the privilege.

Within the temple walls were all the services needed to support the members of the cult, and bakeries, kitchens, workshops, artists' studios and breweries were all literally on site, producing everything from basic

OPPOSITE & LEFT: Coloured papyrus columns in the mortuary temple of Ramesses III, Medinet Habu.

foodstuffs to furniture to a variety of gifts that could be offered to the gods.

The funding of the temple and its support system was, of course, essential; temples liaised closely with the pharaoh, but were able to exercise considerable autonomy in their own right. The temples often had large estates connected with them, where the food and raw materials necessary for the temple and the cult were produced, together with cash crops to bring in extra funding. Typically, these would have consisted of farmland, gardens, orchards, quarries and mines.

Estates were not necessarily situated near or around the temple itself, and land could be granted to a temple in a distant part of Egypt; for example, the temple of Seti I, during the New Kingdom period, acquired land close to the second cataract in Nubia.

As with any centre of population, food had to be harvested and stored. Temple complexes tended to have silos for grain, usually in groups of two to five, scattered around a square courtyard. The silos were usually made from mud or mud brick, and the more remote the temple, the greater was the need to ensure adequate supplies. The grain would obviously be used not only to feed the cult, but also to provide offerings.

FAR LEFT: Statue of the lion-headed goddess Sekhmet in the mortuary temple of Ramesses III.

LEFT: Ramessid column in the temple of Ramesses III.

OPPOSITE: Ruins of the mortuary temple of Seti I at Luxor.

We do not know how this actually worked, but offerings were made to the gods at the granaries themselves. There was, after all, a direct and necessary link between obtaining a bountiful harvest and making sure it was repeated.

Apart from the priests, large numbers of people needed to live in proximity to the temple itself, though some of the priests, officials and administrators lived on the temple estate and occasionally inside the temple itself. Most of the other workers, however, were housed away from the temple in local villages.

There were, of course, many temples in Ancient Egypt and it is a testament to their excellent construction that so many of them have survived. One question always arises: what determined the location of a temple? This was not only a religious consideration, there were other, more practical reasons why a particular place was chosen. Perhaps it was the birthplace of a god, or it may have been associated with a particular myth or legend, or it may have been near a place where an individual, believed to possess particular powers, had been buried. But it could simply be a replacement for an older temple. More often than not, however, it would be near a population centre, or where resources were readily available. A good example of this is the temple of Seti I at Abydos, which required

OPPOSITE: The Temple of Debod was given to Spain in 1968, to save it from being flooded when the Aswan Dam was built. It was re-erected in Madrid.

LEFT: Site of the memorial temple to Queen Hatshepsut, Deir el-Bahri, Luxor.

an Osireion; in other words, it needed a pool of water, so it was located close to a natural spring.

Once a site had been selected, the question of orientation came to the fore. It is clear that most of the temples in the vicinity of the Nile were oriented east to west, which means at right angles to the river, as were the mortuary temples built during the New Kingdom period at Thebes, which although built in fairly quick succession, do not align exactly with one another. Sometimes the alignment of a temple had more to do

OPPOSITE: Temple of Khnum, Esna.

ABOVE: A djed pillar, adorned with armlets and bracelets, holding the crook and flail of royalty. Tomb of Nefertari, Abu Simbel.

RIGHT: The god Khepri, the Great Scarab, also from the tomb of Nefertari.

FAR RIGHT: Relief of Horus in the mortuary temple of Rameses III.

with what was there before. The temples at Luxor and Edfu were built from north to south, mainly because they were replacements of existing structures, while the Temple of Amun at Luxor was built so that it would directly face the main temple at Karnak.

A much later Ptolemaic temple at Edfu was built at right angles to a New Kingdom temple that had fallen into disrepair, the older temple having run from east to west. Even when the Egyptians wanted their temple to face a rising star, they could not always be guaranteed to have made the right calculation. There was a New Kingdom temple to Horus on Thoth Hill, Luxor, that was built to line up with the dog-star Sirius. Unfortunately, between the building of this first temple and the building of its replacement, the orientation of the star had changed.

Another example of astronomical alignment can be found at Abu Simbel. The temple of Ramesses II was designed so that at certain times of the year light would shine through the door of the temple and illuminate the statues of the gods at the back.

Probably the most famous and most visited Egyptian remains are to be found at Karnak, which came to prominence at the beginning of the Middle Kingdom period, and which during the next 2,000 years was restored, enlarged, pulled down and added to by various pharaohs. Incredibly, during the rule of

OPPOSITE: Relief from the mortuary temple of Ramesses III, with the god Khnum as the central figure.

LEFT: Sekhmet, the lion-headed Eye of Re, also from the temple at Medinet Habu.

Ramesses III, 80,000 people worked in the temple and its environs, growing crops and carrying out other essential duties.

The temple at Karnak is built along two axes and has a number of smaller temples and chapels as well as a sacred lake. The northern part is dedicated to the old war god, Mentu, and is the smallest of the three main parts of the temple; as we see it now, it is the most poorly preserved part of the complex. The southern part contains the Temple of Mut, that lies some 900ft (275m) to the south of the temple of Amun-Re. This was the part of the complex that was extensively added to over a period of years, and that possibly ran from the 17th through to the 30th dynasty and beyond.

The temple of Amun-Re itself has a courtyard, topening up behind a pylon, where there is a barque shrine made of granite and sandstone. All the signs are there that various pharaohs lavished time and money on improving and upgrading the temple, there being 20 or more small chapels and temples within the temple precinct.

The final part of the vast complex was the work of Akhenaten, Amenhotep III's successor, who spent the first five years of his reign at Thebes. There, he ordered the construction of five major works, of which only one, the main Aten temple to the east of Thebes, has been located and partially excavated. Then for some inexplicable reason he suddenly abandoned the project

moving his court to Amarna, a new city he had built as his administrative and political capital. From that point on, all work ceased, and the worship of the Aten eventually petered out. By the end of Akhenaten's reign, most of the people had returned to Amun-Re and the old, traditional religion

Today the temples hold as much fascination for tourists as the pyramids and the Valley of the Kings. Many of the key temples lie along well-trodden paths, but others are rather more remote and therefore rarely visited. Even so, many of the sites continue to reveal hitherto unknown artefacts and information concerning the lives of the Ancient Egyptians, and literally hundreds of years of archeological excavation remain to be completed before there is a full understanding of how the temples worked.

There are magnificent examples of temples all around the west bank of the River Nile, in what the Egyptians called Thebes, but which we now know as Luxor-Karnak. Temples created by Amenhotep I lie cheek by jowl, not only with those that Ramesses built, but also with the temples of the would-be pharaohs of the Ptolemaic period.

OPPOSITE: A depiction of the ram-headed god Khnum from the tomb of Nefertari.

ABOVE LEFT: Repeated images of the goddess Nekhbet in vulture form, in the mortuary temple of Ramesses III.

CHAPTER NINE
HIEROGLYPHICS

Early hieroglyphs were stylized pictures of objects, representing a word, syllable or sound, as found in Ancient Egyptian and certain other ancient writing systems, developed to convey the spoken word. But the Egyptians had gone one further and had created a system that could be used either phonetically, where each hieroglyph represented a vocal sound, or ideogrammatically, where the idea of a thing was symbolized, without indicating the sounds needed to verbalize it.

Eventually, an abridged form of hieroglyphics was used, known as hieratic script, which allowed faster writing on papyrus. This probably continued until 600 BC or so, and was used primarily by the priesthood in religious, literary, and business texts. By around 700 BC, a second form had evolved, known as demotic, that would be replaced by Greek in the Ptolemaic Period. In its final stages, these early Egyptian scripts came together in the language of the Christian Copts, which

LEFT: Hieroglyphs in the Temple of Hathor at Dendera.

OPPOSITE: A modern interpretation of the Ancient Egyptian alphabet, drawn on papyrus.

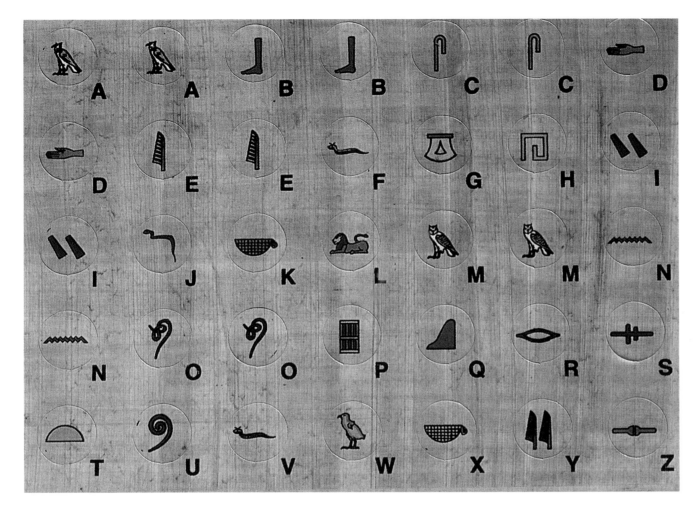

the Egyptians called *medu netjer*, and which allowed the secret of hieroglyphs to be eventually revealed. Sadly, by the 5th century AD, very few people knew how to read or write the old scripts.

Over the centuries, various attempts were made to decipher hieroglyphics. It was realized that each hieroglyph had a specific meaning, some of the objects depicted being recognizable, but the exact meaning of each pictogram continued to elude. Hieroglyphs were believed to be symbolic, imbued with secret meanings,

which at that point, were beyond the understanding of those studying them at that time; many sought the key whereby the secret would be unlocked. They would have a long time to wait, as it turned out, because this did not happen until the 18th and 19th centuries AD.

Working in the 17th century, a Jesuit, Athanasius Kircher, who by all accounts was an accomplished linguist and a man of many talents, made some progress towards understanding hieroglyphics, though his work was later discredited. He had compiled the

first Coptic grammar and vocabulary, which was by then the spoken and written language of the Egyptian people; he recognized that Coptic was not a separate language, but a development of Ancient Egyptian. Although he could not have known it, this knowledge would be vital when the Rosetta Stone was discovered.

In 1785, Jean Barthélémy formed the opinion that some hieroglyphs related to royal or divine names, but the breakthrough came in July 1799. Napoleon, at the head of a French invading army, had set up camp in the Nile delta, close to a place called Rosetta. Here, soldiers discovered a large, black basalt stone, 11in thick, 3ft 9in tall and 2ft 4in wide, which seemed to be a fragment of a larger piece, as much as 6ft (2m) tall. It had inscriptions in three languages, hieroglyphics, demotic and Greek. The stone was sent to Alexandria, and specialists at Napoleon's headquarters began to examine the stone. Copies of the inscriptions were made by making rubbings of them, and these were sent to other specialists throughout Europe.

Ultimately the French were defeated and thrown out of Egypt by the British. The Rosetta Stone was sent to London, where it was given pride of place in the British Museum, where it remains to this day.

Stephen Weston found no difficulty in translating the Greek text in 1902, and discovered that the stone dated to 196 BC, which was during the reign of Ptolemy V. It was a decree by the general council of priests that recorded honours bestowed on the king by various temples. It was then realized that the Greek was a direct translation of the hieroglyphic and demotic texts, and the possibility of decipherment seemed imminent. The first step was to match the names of individuals mentioned in the Greek text with the hieroglyphs, and

of 29 letters. As it would turn out, however, he was only half right. Although he had been able to identify basic words, such as 'him', 'Greek' and 'temple', Akerblad made the mistake of believing that demotic was an alphabet, when it was phonetic, and was unable to proceed much further.

Thomas Young continued the task in 1814. He had acquired fragments of papyri and was certain that demotic was not alphabetic. He managed to isolate particular groups of symbols, which represented individual words, comparing them with the Greek,

OPPOSITE: A relief with figures and hieroglyphs, Karnak.

FAR LEFT: These hieroglyphs appear in the Avenue of the Cryocephalous Rams, leading to the west gate of the Karnak temple complex.

ABOVE: Hieroglyphs from the Temple of Semna, Aswan, built by Tuthmose III in honour of Senusret III and the Nubian god Dedwen.

Sylvestre de Sacy managed to identify the names of Ptolemy and Alexander, before he hit a brick wall.

A Swedish diplomat and student of de Sacy, Johan Akerblad, continued the work and was able to identify several of the demotic names and built up an alphabet

hieroglyphic signs. He also found that the groups of hieroglyphs contained within ovals or cartouches were royal names. After a year or so, Young had created a vocabulary of 86 words, which directly associated the demotic with the Greek.

The next individual to become involved was Jean-François Champollion, who corrected and enlarged Young's list of hieroglyphs. Champollion worked on the basis of isolating names that had several common hieroglyphs, which he could then check against other sets of hieroglyphs, enabling him to identify the names of Roman emperors who had ruled Egypt.

Purely by chance, a tourist had brought an obelisk back to Britain. The obelisk and its base block had been found in the Temple of Philae, near Aswan, and on the base were the royal names of Ptolemy and Cleopatra, written in Greek. Also on the obelisk were two cartouches bearing the royal names. Champollion compared it with the hieroglyphs on the Rosetta Stone and found that they matched.

More information then came his way, including copies of inscriptions and reliefs, some of which had cartouches with names repeated in different ways. He was thus able to identify other Egyptian rulers, but unfortunately died in 1832 and others were left to continue his work.

realizing that some characters had corresponding hieroglyphs that had been intermingled with letters of an alphabet. He was also able to draw on other information, including new papyri and funeral rolls, which had been brought from Egypt. He discovered that the Egyptian language was not a single set of characters, but in fact two, hieratic and demotic, that would make it possible to match demotic and

FAR LEFT: Obelisk of Hatshepsut, Karnak.

ABOVE LEFT: Hieroglyphs in the Temple of Luxor.

OPPOSITE TOP: A papyrus with hieroglyphs, describing Queen Nefertari's passage to the Afterlife.

When Egyptians wrote hieroglyphs, it was common practice to write each one in a rectangular or square area, and sometimes there would be more than one hieroglyph in the same area. Secondary hieroglyphs were usually smaller, so an area could contain a large hieroglyph and several smaller ones.

Confusingly, hieroglyphs can be read in different directions, depending on the way they are arranged. What was eventually realized is that a hieroglyph in which an animal is shown facing a particular way indicates that it is read in the opposite direction. A further complication is when there are two hieroglyphs in the same area, when the uppermost should be read first, followed by those underneath. Some hieroglyphs are set out in rows or columns: rows are read in the correct direction, downwards, while columns are always read across.

The Egyptians did not use their language in the same way as us. Not only did they use an alphabet, they also used signs that indicated combinations of sounds. By and large, vowels were ignored.

However we choose to pronounce hieroglyphs, we do not know how the Egyptians themselves actually pronounced them. They used some symbols as consonant signs, but if they were placed close to the vowels 'i' or 'u' they became semi-vowels. Here is a basic vocabulary of hieroglyphs commonly found in Egyptian buildings and on Egyptian artefacts.

HIEROGLYPH	SOUND	TRANSLITERATION	MEANINGS
	m	em	1. in 2. by means of, with (of instrument) 3. from, out of
	n	en	1. to, for (in sense of dative) 2. to (of direction, only to persons)
	r	er	1. to, into, towards (of direction towards things) 2. in respect of
	pn	pen	1. this (masculine) Follows the noun
	tn	pen	1. this (feminine) Follows the noun
	ky	key	1. other, another (masculine) Precedes the noun
	kt	ket	1. other, another (feminine) Precedes the noun
	ym	yem	1. there, therein, therewith, therefrom

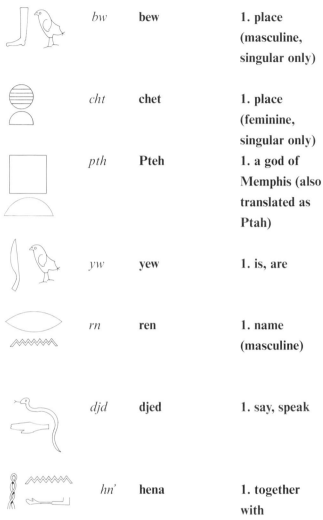

bw	**bew**	1. place (masculine, singular only)
cht	**chet**	1. place (feminine, singular only)
pth	**Pteh**	1. a god of Memphis (also translated as Ptah)
yw	**yew**	1. is, are
rn	**ren**	1. name (masculine)
djd	**djed**	1. say, speak
hn'	**hena**	1. together with

LEFT: Hieroglyphs found at Karnak.

OPPOSITE ABOVE: More examples of hieroglyphs taken from the Obelisk of Hatshepsut, Karnak.

Ideograms, or sense signs, were used to convey meaning pictorially and were often accompanied by phonograms. The way in which the phonograms are used, or the order in which they appear, can give different meanings to the same sets of symbols, such as in the following example, which features the circular sign for the sun.

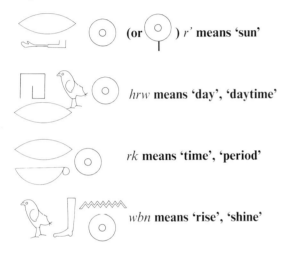

(or) *r'* means 'sun'

hrw means 'day', 'daytime'

rk means 'time', 'period'

wbn means 'rise', 'shine'

Some of the ideograms end a word and in these cases they are known as determinatives, the reason for this being that the ideogram determines the meaning of the sound sign it follows. There are a number of generic determinatives, which are used to express the sense of the words rather than their specific meaning. The following are ideal examples:

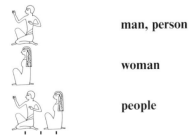

man, person

woman

people

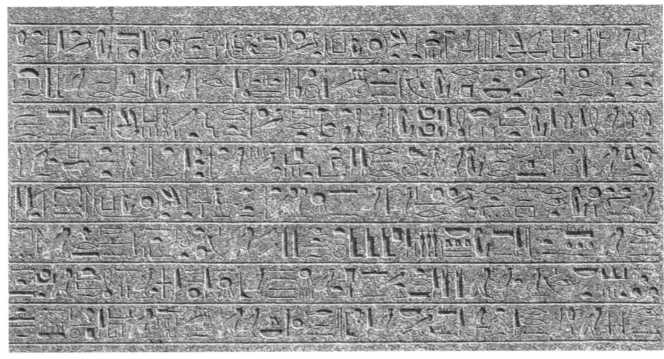

old man, old, lean on		praise, supplicate	
official, man in authority		force, effort	
exalted person, the dead		eat, drink, speak, think, feel	
god, king		lift, carry	
king		weary, weak	
goddess, queen (or)		enemy, foreigner	
high, rejoice, support		enemy, death	

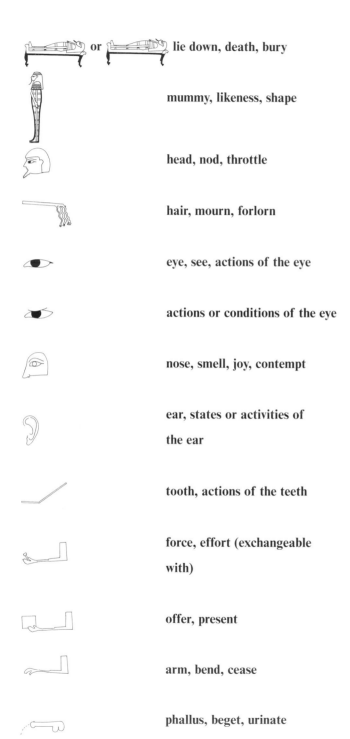

or — lie down, death, bury

mummy, likeness, shape

head, nod, throttle

hair, mourn, forlorn

eye, see, actions of the eye

actions or conditions of the eye

nose, smell, joy, contempt

ear, states or activities of the ear

tooth, actions of the teeth

force, effort (exchangeable with)

offer, present

arm, bend, cease

phallus, beget, urinate

leg, foot, actions of the feet

walk, run

move backwards

tumours, odours, disease

bodily discharges

cattle

savage

skin, mammal

bird, insect

small, bad, weak

fish

snake, worm

tree

LEFT: Hieroglyphs within cartouches from Saqqara.

OPPOSITE: Wall paintings and hieroglyphs at Gurna, Luxor.

	plant, flower
or	vine, fruit, garden
	wood, tree
or	corn, grain
	sky, above
	sun, light, time
	night, darkness
	star
	fire, heat, cook
	air, wind, sail
	stone
	copper, bronze
	sand, minerals, pellets
	water, liquid, actions
	connected with water

OPPOSITE LEFT: Papyrus showing Maat, the Lady of Truth, Justice and Order.

ABOVE: Hieroglyphs from a temple at Buhen, built by Hatshepsut and re-built by her stepson, Tuthmose III.

RIGHT: Intricate hieroglyphs found at Dendera.

sheet of water

irrigated land

land

road, travel, position

desert, foreign country

foreign (country or person)

town, village, Egypt

house, building

door, open

box, coffin

shrine, palanquin, mat

boat, ship, navigation

sacred barque

clothe, linen

bind, document

rope, actions with cord or rope

knife, cut

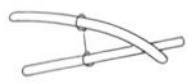

hoe, cultivate, hack up

break, divide, cross

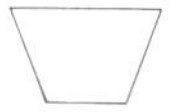

cup

vessel, anoint

or    pot, vessel, beverages

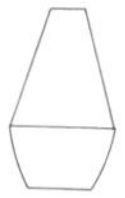

bread, cake

or 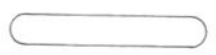   loaf, cake, offering

festival

or   book, writing, abstract
older form

royal name, king

one; the object depicted

| | also ⦙ , | | | , ○○○ several, plural

\   substitute for signs difficult to
draw (not often used)

OPPOSITE: Hieroglyphs on a stele at Karnak.

ABOVE: Hieroglyphs, Karnak.

Biliteral signs were also a part of Egyptian writing and were, in effect, the combination of two consonants. The following set of hieroglyphs all use the letter 'a, as the second consonant.

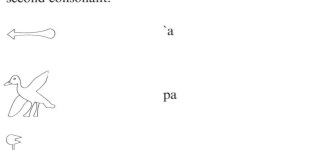 `a

pa

cha

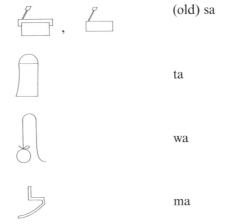 (old) sa

ta

wa

ma

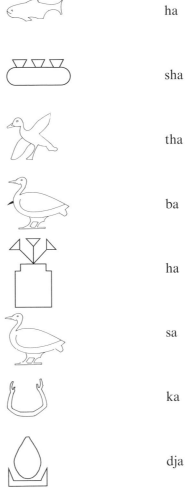 ha

sha

tha

ba

ha

sa

ka

dja

OPPOSITE: A hunting scene with the goddess Bastet depicted as a lioness. She was often linked with Artemis, the Greek goddess of hunting.

ABOVE LEFT: Catching cattle, a painting on papyrus.

PAGES 324–325: Vegetation, such as reeds, grasses and papyrus, grows prolifically along the banks of the Nile.

The set of eight illustrations on this and the following pages show how papyrus is made.

Egyptian writing was, in essence, the union of two major inventions, the first being the script itself, which consisted of signs representing words or sounds common in human speech; the second was the technological development that allowed the written language to be transmitted and recorded.

The Ancient Egyptians made extensive use of paper made from the papyrus reed, and are believed to have used it some 2,000 years before the Chinese invented paper made from vegetable pulp. The Egyptians had the first manufacturing process by which they could make high-quality writing material. The papyrus reed (*Cyperus papyrus*) is a wetland sedge, once abundant in the Nile delta, but now extinct in the north. But in Ancient Egypt the papyrus was a common plant and could be used for many different purposes. The plant could grow to a height of 25ft (8m) or so and had thick, triangular stems, with a

fibrous outer covering, and soft, spongy, pith-like tissue inside. The outer covering was used for making ropes, sandals, mats and cloth, while the pith could be eaten, either raw or cooked. Neither were the roots of the plant ignored, but used for fuel or to make household utensils, while the papyrus stems, being buoyant, could be lashed together to create simple reed boats. But it was the use of papyrus as a writing material that would revolutionize the Egyptian language.

The outer covering was first removed from the papyrus stems and the stems soaked in water. Then the sticky, fibrous inner pith was cut lengthwise into thin strips, which were laid out side by side. They were then placed, usually overlapping, on a piece of cloth on top of a hard, level surface. Strips of pith would continue to be added at right angles to the first layer, so that they overlapped and formed a continuous sheet. A second piece of cloth was then placed over the pith

layers, and was beaten using a mallet or a piece of wood. It is thought that the strips may have been soaked in water long enough for decomposition to begin, perhaps increasing adhesion, but this is not known for sure. But the process would have separated the papyrus fibres and extracted the starch from the pith, which would have held the fibres together. This was obviously a skilled operation, and workers had to ensure that vertical and horizontal fibres were kept

correctly in place. After the beating process had been completed, the papyrus sheet was left out in the sun to dry, after which time its surface would be polished with a smooth stone. The sheets were used to make a long scroll, the largest of which is known as the Great Harris Papyrus, which is a staggering 135ft (41m) long.

Another reed, *Juncus maritimus*, was used to make writing implements. A ten-inch section of the reed was cut and the tip was then sliced at an angle; this was then crushed or chewed to create a fine brush. Typically, the Egyptians used a finely-ground red ochre, a natural earthy pigment, to create red ink, and carbon or fine soot was used to make black.

The basic ink was mixed with gum before being shaped into small cakes, which were then dried, ready to be placed on the scribe's palette. Before writing, the reed brush would be dipped into water, then rubbed onto the surface of the ink block. Over a period of time, additional colours would have been added that enabled more colourful hieroglyphs to be created.

Hieroglyphics are not only found on papyrus. They were also applied to blocks of wood, covered with a gum mixture, while others have been found on pottery and limestone. This is, of course, in addition to the many hieroglyphs that discovered on wooden objects, such as coffins, and delicately carved into the stone on the walls of tombs and other ancient buildings and sculptures.

Many of the papyrus texts have survived due to their careful storage and the fact that they were kept in conditions where there was little moisture. One of the best-preserved papyrus texts is 78ft (24m) long and can be found in the British Museum. The Book of the Dead, as it is known, was prepared for the scribe Ani, who died in 1400 BC.

The production of papyrus eventually became a state monopoly, though Egyptians were quite prepared to export their paper to other countries, fragments of it having been found in Greece, Asia, Mesopotamia and other parts of Europe. But due to different climatic conditions, very little has actually survived outside Egypt, though huge amounts of papyrus texts have been found in the ancient towns, cities and necropolis cemeteries of Egypt.

OPPOSITE: This painted papyrus is a protective amulet. It depicts the goddess Nekhbet, in the guise of a vulture, and Wadjet, a snake goddess associated with the land, placed either side of the Eye of Horus.

Bible, witten on papyrus or dried animal skins. They are of great religious and historical significance, being the only known surviving Biblical documents written before AD 100.

A large number of papyri began to leave Egypt during the latter half of the 18th century, the first recorded sale taking place in 1778, when an antiques dealer purchased papyri dating from AD 191. At the beginning of the 19th century, many papyri from Elephantine, Thebes, Memphis and other places throughout Middle and Upper Egypt, found their way to Europe, where they still lie in various museums.

It is obvious that not all papyri were valuable, and many were simply thrown away; some, however, were recycled and used for other purposes. Pieces of papyrus were sometimes used to wrap up mummified corpses, before they were covered in plaster and painted in bright colours. By far the greatest number of papyri to have survived come from the Greek and Roman periods, the vast majority dating from the 4th century BC to the 7th century AD. A large number of these papyri have texts written in Greek, which was the administrative language for a considerable time, following the conquest of Egypt by Alexander the Great, and persisted even through the period of Roman rule and the later Arab conquest.

The Dead Sea scrolls, found in Israel, are early Christian documents, including texts from the Hebrew

A huge number, perhaps hundreds of thousands of sheets, were discovered at El Fayoum in 1877, believed to be the site of the ancient City of Crocodiles, and there have been other important finds since then. Of the estimated 400,000 papyri still in public and private collections around the world, only 50,000 have ever been published.

Towards the end of the 7th century AD, a version of our modern paper begun to appear in Europe, and this is when the Egyptians stopped exporting papyrus. The Arab conquest heralded the introduction of pulp paper, and although it may have been less durable, it was far less expensive. Over time, therefore, Egypt ceased to produce papyrus, the plantations fell into disuse, and the plant itself all but disappeared from Egypt.

The tradition was revived in the 1960s, when Dr. Hassan Ragab reintroduced the papyrus plant from the Sudan and established a plantation and Pharaonic Village near Cairo. Although not familiar with Ancient Egyptian methods of papyrus production, he experimented himself and managed to work out how

OPPOSITE LEFT: A prince and princess, cruising the celestial Nile (the sky) in the solar barque.

OPPOSITE RIGHT: A tree of life painted on papyrus.

LEFT: Painting with hieroglyphs, depicting Re as a cat slaying Apep, the Great Destroyer. Apep was a huge serpent or crocodile, living in the waters of Nu or in the celestial Nile, which every day attempted to disrupt the passage of Re's solar barque. Deir el-Medina.

LEFT & ABOVE: Hieroglyphs found in the Temple of Semna West, built by Tuthmose III. National Museum, Khartoum.

OPPOSITE: The Island of Philae, by David Roberts, c.1836.

it was done by studying descriptions of the process provided by travellers in Ancient Egypt. The art of papyrus-making is now very much a feature of modern Egyptian tourism and trade.

Nowadays, papyrus is generally used in decorative art, produced in large quantities, but still not on an industrial scale. It is often difficult to distinguish forgeries from the genuine article, though older papyri are difficult to tear and are usually strong and weighty. They also tended to have pronounced colour variations, and brown veins can be seen when they are held up to the light.

Different grades of papyri were made in Ancient Egypt, the finest quality coming from the pith at the

ABOVE LEFT: Philae, seen from the South, by David Roberts, 1838.

ABOVE: Detail on one of the Colossi of Memnon.

OPPOSITE: Relief from the Temple of Hathor, Dendera.

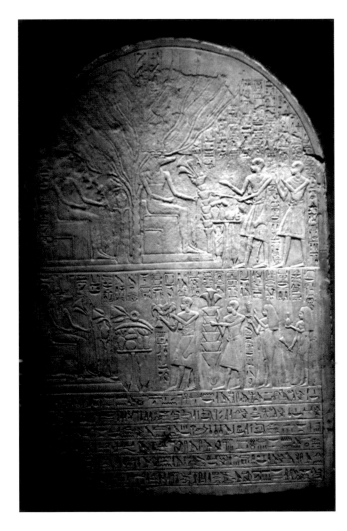

ABOVE: Stele dedicated to Sobek, Luxor museum.

RIGHT: The Temple of Dendur, dating from Egypt's Roman period. It came under threat following the building of the Aswan Dam, when it was given to the Metropolitan Museum of Art, New York. It was re-erected in the Sackler Wing in 1978.

OPPOSITE: Part of the Buhen temple in the National Museum, Khartoum.

It was not an easy profession to master, there being literally hundreds of different hieroglyphs to memorize. The scribes were taught the hieratic script and would have known how to create hieroglyphs with dexterity, using a minimum of brushstrokes. Even though writing down information was their main task, they were also expected to keep an enormous amount of knowledge in their heads.

As we have seen, papyrus probably came into general manufacture in around 3100 BC, which coincided with a burgeoning bureaucracy in Egypt. The Egyptians would continue to use scribes in this and many other contexts for many generations to come.

Scribes, when they were being trained, were not allowed to use papyrus, due to the complexity and expense of its production, but used broken pieces of pottery instead. It is believed that future scribes began their formal education at the age of nine and would probably have been proficient and ready to start work by the time they were 12.

Training was strict and the only school for scribes known to have existed was at Deir el-Medina. Here, students were expected to copy passages from the hieroglyphic text known as the Book of Kemyt. After this, they would progress to classical works of literature, poetry, and the creation of model letters, before tackling various other writing tasks set by their teachers.

LEFT and OPPOSITE: Hieroglyphs from the Temple of Luxor.

PAGES 342 & 343: Views of Deir el-Medina, a village that once supplied workers for the Valley of the Kings..

CHAPTER TEN
EGYPTIAN MYTHS

CHAPTER TEN
EGYPTIAN MYTHS

Much like the systems of religion that exist today, while the Ancient Egyptians may all have believed in a god or gods, not all of them found agreement in the details of their religion. Different classes of individuals, living in Ancient Egypt over an enormously lengthy period of time, held different shades of belief, and the view of the gods held by an Egyptian peasant may have been very different from that of a pharaoh or priest. The idea that beings superior to mere mortals could actually exist, developed in Predynastic Egypt, and spread throughout the population by word of mouth or Egyptian writings.

The gods bore a resemblance to the human race, in that they were born, had their own individual characteristics, fought, loved, and then died. What tended to confuse was that many of them were interchangeable and tended to overlap one with the other to a large extent. The importance of a particular god at a particular time depended largely on the personal beliefs of the current pharaoh, and the way he chose to worship his gods would not have extended far beyond his capital. As a result of this, the myths and legends of Ancient Egypt were subject to mutations: locations were swapped, and individual gods became known by a variety of other names.

Gods could have many associations and consequently as many names, some of which were simply descriptive, reflecting the personal attributes of the god. It is no wonder, therefore, that the identity of the supreme creator tended to differ, changing from Atum, Re and Amun in some places, to Ptah, Khnum and even the Aten elsewhere. The heavens were represented by Bat, Horus and Nut, among others, while Osiris and Geb were gods of the earth.

The creation myth is complicated, and several different versions of it were current in Ancient Egypt at different times. All, however, have certain elements in common. The Egyptians believed creation began when a hill rose from a stagnant, lifeless ocean, known as Nu. But different viewpoints held it was the temple of their particular creator that stood on this hill: in fact, the early step pyramids were supposed to be symbolic of this mound. Creation, thereafter, was a relatively slow process. and was not achieved overnight. But

LEFT: Amenhotep II, from the Temple of Amun at Karnak, now in the Luxor museum.

OPPOSITE: Statue of Amun, Temple of Amun, Karnak.

time would eventually come when the gods began to roam the earth.

Atum, the primeval sun god, whose aspect was the setting sun, was worshipped particularly at Heliopolis, the site of the Ennead cult. Egyptians following the Heliopolitan version of the creation, believed that Atum had been the prime mover. Atum was later syncretized with Re as the god Atum-Re, symbolized by the phoenix. According to the myth, Atum was the first substance (a hill) to have emerged from the primeval waters. Atum's children may either have been born on the primeval hill, or created in the waters of Nu. Atum gave birth to his son, Shu, by spitting him out, then vomited forth his daughter, Tefnut. Shu and Tefnut continued the process of creation by establishing a social order, to which Shu contributed life, while Tefnut established order.

The twins later became separated from their father and lost their way in Nu's watery chaos. Atum had only one eye, which he removed, sending it in search of his children, who eventually returned with the eye. Atum accordingly wept tears joy, and it was from these tears that mankind was born. Shu and Tefnut subsequently became the parents of Geb, the earth, and Nut, the sky, who in turn gave birth to Osiris, Isis, Set and Nephthys. With Horus, the son of Osiris and Isis, these nine gods formed the Ennead of Heliopoliss.

An alternative view of creation originated in the city of Memphis, which, by 3100 BC, was the capital of Upper and Lower Egypt. Here, Ptah was believed to be the creator, the other gods being simply various aspects of his godhead, including the stagnant ocean, Nu.

The third version of events came from Hermopolis, where a group of eight gods were recognized, known as

the Ogdoad. These were the paired Nun and Naunet, Huh and Hauhet, Kuk and Kauket, Amun and Amaunet, who ruled the earth, dying after a time, when they became part of the Underworld. Each pair represented an aspect of the universe: Nun and Naunet water, Huh and Hauhet unendingness, Kuk and Kauket darkness, and Amun and Amaunet air.

In the Middle Kingdom, when Thebes began to grow in importance, its patron, Amun, also became more significant, as did his wife, Amaunet, who was simply a female aspect of Amun. Amaunet was replaced with a more substantial mother-goddess, namely Mut, and Amun, Mut and their son, Khonsu, were known thereafter as the Theban Triad. The Thebans also believed their city to be the exemplar against which all others should be measured.

Amun had no parents, and as creator of the universe, therefore created himself. According to this legend, Amun spat out Shu, then vomited out Tefnut. Shu and Tefnut eventually gave birth to Geb and Nut, and the other gods followed on as before.

Previously mentioned in connection with Atum, was the phoenix, a mythical creature also known as the Benu bird. The Egyptians believed it travelled from Arabia to Heliopolis once every 500 years. Over time, the phoenix came to represent the soul of Osiris, and was also associated with Venus, or the morning star.

LEFT: Painting of Ptah the Creator, in the tomb of Nefertari.

OPPOSITE: Osiris and Atum, also in the tomb of Nefertari.

Although these creation stories differ slightly, all Egyptians believed their daily temple rituals to be correct, and they all venerated the falcon – associated with the god Horus. Originally, Horus was viewed as a hunting god, then a war god, and finally as a god of the sky. The pharaohs borrowed heavily on this symbolism, believing the falcon to be a symbol of their power. Some believed that temples were originally designed as perches or shelters for falcons, and symbolic perches in temples were often to be seen.

By recognizing the similarities, however, we arrive at a composite version of events, or what is known as the Delta Cycle, which goes something like this.

There was a time when the gods roamed the earth, principal among them being Nu, Atum, Re, Shu, Tefnut, Geb, Nut and Osiris. In addition to these was the god Set, the son of Geb and Nut, who was later to be regarded as the embodiment of evil. From his very birth, when he ripped himself from his mother's womb, Set had been a violent god, and he was to murder his brother, Osiris, to gain power. Some of the other gods were so terrified of him during the period of his rule, that they hid themselves inside the bodies of animals.

LEFT: Thoth, the god of wisdom, from the Temple of Sobek and Haroeris, Kom Ombo.

OPPOSITE LEFT: Geb, the earth god, Kom Ombo.

OPPOSITE RIGHT: Set, god of evil, from the tomb of Amunherkhepshep, Valley of the Queens, Luxor.

Isis was captured by Set, her brother, after he had murdered her husband and brother, Osiris. But she managed to escape, hiding in a swamp in the Nile delta. By now, Isis was carrying Osiris's child, Horus, who would eventually avenge his father's murder. As Horus grew up, the other gods and nymphs kept a careful eye on him to make sure he was not captured or harmed by Set, and even Set's wife and sister, Nephthys, decided to abandon her husband to help protect the child. Being the embodiment of Set himself, it was necessary to be especially vigilant against snakes; however, the unthinkable happened, and Horus was bitten, though, fortunately, the gods were able to combine their power to save him.

Once Horus had grown to maturity, he emerged from the swamp to claim his rightful place as Osiris's son. What happened next is referred to as the Great Quarrel, when the Council of the Gods, being unable to decide who the principal god should be, now that Osiris was dead, engaged in a long and bitter debate. At last, the gods reluctantly chose Set, he being the stronger character, but eventually, after 80 years had passed, the crown was given to Horus. Set was beside himself with rage, as a result of this, and challenged Horus to a fight to the death. Fierce fighting in the sea ensued, both parties in the guise of hippopotamuses.

LEFT: The Temple of Amun, Siwa. Alexander the Great visited the oracle here in 331 BC.

RIGHT: Relief of Atum, Kom Ombo.

PAGES 358–359: Temple of Isis, Philae, Aswan.

Isis became involved in the struggle, making matters worse by accidentally harpooning Horus, whom she immediately released. She then harpooned Set, who managed to persuade Isis to let him go. This annoyed Horus so much, that he rose up out of the water and cut off his mother's head. Horus then fled, rather than be punished by the gods for his heinous crime, reaching safety in an oasis, where he could not be found.

Set was determined to find him, however, and when he did, he ripped out Horus's eyes, thrusting them into the earth, where lotus flowers appeared. Set then abandoned Horus, denying he had ever found him. One of the other gods was not convinced, however, and Hanthor went to find Horus, giving him back his eyes; he brought Horus before the gods, demanding there be a truce.

But Set was not to be deterred and challenged Horus to a boat race. Horus built his boat from wood that very night, giving it a layer of gypsum. Set, when he saw it, believed it to be made of stone, so he built

OPPOSITE & PAGES 362–363: Ruins of the Temple of Satis, Elephantine island, Aswan.

ABOVE RIGHT: The Four Sons of Horus, in the tomb of Setnakht and Tausert in the Valley of the Queens, Luxor.

PAGE 364: Ptah the Creator, the Great Temple of Re-Harakhte, Abu Simbel.

PAGE 365: A painting illustrating an incident from the Book of the Dead, from the tomb of Menna, Valley of the Nobles.

his own boat from what he thought was the same material. Once the race was under way, Set's boat sank. He was so angry that Horus had been able to fool him, that he tried to attack him again, but was prevented from doing so by the gods. It was now obvious that Horus should remain king, and by way of compensation, Set was made the god of storms.

It was believed in Egypt, however, that the two were destined to fight until the end of time, when *maat* would be destroyed and the waters of Nu (chaos) would engulf the earth. Now that Set had been labelled the epitome of evil, it was necessary that Horus win the ultimate battle, making sure that good was triumphant. The feud between Set and Horus has been seen in some quarters as symbolic of the struggle to unite Egypt. According to this theory, the followers of Horus were therefore successful, and Set was accordingly pushed further into the background.

Being a follower of Set or Seth, it was normal for the Pharaoh Seth-Peribsen to display his name in a *serekh* topped by a Set animal, rather than the usual Horus falcon. On the other hand, Pharaoh

the land where Sekhmet was planning her next attack. When she arrived the following day, no one was in sight. She began to drink what she thought was blood, drinking so much that she could no longer move; eventually, she managed to crawl back to Re, having killed not a single human being.

Re greeted her, deciding that from henceforth she would be called Hathor, and that she would subjugate mankind only through the power of love. Re had managed to save mankind, even though he knew his time on earth was coming to an end. He was aware that he would soon have to pass the mantle of power onto the younger gods.

Re became so old that he began to dribble. Isis took some of his saliva and fashioned it into a cobra, eventually to become the uraeus, the protective symbol destined to be worn by the pharaohs. Isis dropped the cobra onto the ground, knowing that Re would be sure to meet it as he wandered from Upper to Lower Egypt. Sure enough, the cobra bit him, the venom getting into his bloodstream so that he could neither speak nor move. This confused him, because he believed himself to be invulnerable; the only one with the power to harm him was the one who knew his secret name.

Isis was known to be a healer and the queen of magic, who could breathe life into the dying. She told

everything on the earth, the last thing being the human race, or the first inhabitants of Egypt. After that, he transformed himself into a man, becoming the first pharaoh and ruling for thousands of years.

Because he was now mortal, Re began to age and men ceased to fear him. This made the god angry, particularly when he saw his laws being flouted. He called together Shu, Tefnut, Geb, Nut and Nu, describing to them the plots against him, and asked for their advice before he destroyed mankind. Nu advised him to send Sekhmet, a lion-headed goddess of war

and destruction, who had been created from the fire in Re's eye. She subsequently roamed Upper and Lower Egypt, slaughtering all those who had disobeyed Re. For days, the River Nile ran red with so much blood, that even Sekhmet's feet became stained. Re looked at the destruction he had wrought on mankind and regretted what he had done, though he was unable to stop Sekhmet; this could only be achieved through his own cunning.

Re brought together 7,000 jars of beer and blood-red ochre, mixing them together and pouring them over

ABOVE LEFT: Khafre the Great Potter (left), in the tomb of Amoun Har-Khosef, Valley of the Queens.

OPPOSITE: The jackal-headed god Anubis. The mummy in the boat is making its journey to the Underworld. Tomb of Menna, the Valley of the Nobles.

Re that the creature that had harmed him had been created by himself, and that only by telling her his secret name would she be able to save him. Re fell for the trick and told her, but instead of uttering his secret name, Isis remained silent. The poison continued to do its work until Re finally agreed to let his name of power be known; this was on the condition that Isis used it only to save the son she would eventually bear. This was how Isis was able to save Horus, when in another episode, Horus was bitten by Set in the guise of a snake. The oath was sworn and the name of power passed to Isis. Then she cured Re.

Re decided not to continue his earthly reign, but to take his place in the heavens, where, as the sun, he would travel across the sky in a boat.

In 1890, a rock, bearing the story of Egypt's seven-year famine, was discovered on the island of Sahal by Charles Wilbour. The story begins during the 18th year of the rule of Pharaoh Tcheser, a king of the third dynasty. The pharaoh had become most concerned that for the past seven years the Nile had failed to flood, with the result that food was now in short supply. People had begun to steal from one another, indicating that starvation was now making them desperate.

This reminded the pharaoh of a story of how the god Imhotep, the son of Ptah, had delivered Egypt from a similar famine. This led him to inquire which god or goddess was in charge of the Nile and where it rose. From Mater, the high official who ruled over the island of Elephantine and Nubia, he discovered that the Nile began to flood at Elephantine, the precise spot being a double cavern known as the Couch of the Nile, where it was believed the Nile god watched and waited for the time of inundation to begin; when the moment

arrived, he would be transformed into a vigorous young man, who would bring water to all of Egypt. The guardian of the flood was called Khnum (Khenmu) and his job was to open the floodgates only when necessary. Khnum was one of the oldest of the Egyptian gods, his symbol being the flat-horned ram. He is often depicted as a ram-headed man, but he was originally a water god, shown in this guise with water flowing over his hands, and with a jug, wedged between ram's horns, on his head.

Khnum had a temple at Elephantine, which the king determined to visit himself, where he would make offerings to the god. Eventually, the god appeared before him, complaining that his shrine had been left in a state of disrepair. The pharaoh decreed that provided the god promised to continue to make the Nile rise each year, more land on Elephantine would be set aside to enlarge the god's temple, and a new priesthood would be established.

The original decree was apparently written down on wood, but it was later carved into stone and kept in a prominent place, so that no one would ever forget the sacred promise that had been made.

This tale demonstrates how the Ancient Egyptians relied on the Nile, for without the periodic flooding of the land, nothing would have grown. There were obviously times when the Nile failed to flood, and it would have been natural for the Egyptians to assume they had offended the god; this could happen in other situations, and it was believed that only appeasement of the gods would make them relent and answer the people's prayers.

Many of the myths involve either the pharaoh himself or members of his family. A prime example of

this is contained in the story of the hunt for the Book of Thoth, set in the period when Ramesses the Great was pharaoh of Egypt.

Ramesses had several sons and most of them were content to hunt and lead their father's armies into battle. But one of them was more interested in study and contemplation. His name was Setna and he had made it his life's work to understand the ancient scripts. He taught himself to read the inscriptions on temple walls, and was himself a proficient scribe. It is said he was also a magician, and had learned his art from ancient magical texts that even the most learned of the priests had been unable to decipher.

One day, Setna came across a story of another pharaoh's son, who had lived several hundred years before. This individual was called Nefrekeptah and he too had been a great scribe and magician. Nefrekeptah had studied the Book of Thoth, from which he received the power to enchant and understand the languages of all creatures. The story also told how the Book of Thoth had been buried with Nefrekeptah, and that his tomb was at Memphis.

Setna became obsessed with the story and asked his brother, Anherru, to help him to find the book. The brothers headed for Memphis and found the tomb of Nefrekeptah, the son of Amenhotep. Setna broke into the tomb and headed for the central chamber, where he found the body of the dead prince lying mummified inside. On the stone sarcophagus sat two ghostly figures, one a young woman and the other a boy.

Resting on Nefrekeptah's chest was the Book of Thoth. Setna was aware that the ghostly presences were protecting the body. He spoke to them, telling them who he was and why he had come. He told them that he

wished to take the Book of Thoth in peace, but that he would use force or magic if they resisted. Their reply was that the book would bring him nothing but misfortune. The female then told Setna that she had been the wife and sister of Nefrekeptah and that they had had a son, Merab. Her husband had become obsessed with ancient writings and magic, his priests having told him that the only text worth reading was the Book of Thoth. It was reputed to contain the wisdom of the gods, which would be bestowed on anyone possessing it. Nefrekeptah demanded to know where the book was hidden, but the priest demanded 100 bars of silver for his funeral and the promise that he would be buried like a pharaoh, before he would divulge his secret.

Nefrekeptah agreed, and the priest told him that the book lay in an iron box beneath the River Nile at Koptos. Inside the iron box, successive boxes of bronze, sycamore, ivory, ebony, silver and gold had to be opened before the Book of Thoth would eventually be revealed. The problem was that the iron box was covered in snakes and scorpions, and that its ultimate protection was a serpent that could never be killed. Nefrekeptah was not deterred, however, and with the pharaoh's permission sailed to Koptos in the royal boat, taking with him his wife, Ahura, and his son, Merab.

As they sailed up the Nile, they were met by worshippers of Isis. Nefrekeptah made sacrifices to Isis and Horus, and on the fifth day began to cast magic spells. The first thing he was able to conjure up was a magic cabin, filled with men and equipment, which he sank into the river; then he filled up the royal boat with sand and anchored it in the middle of the Nile. The men in the cabin, kept alive by magic, started to dig up

the riverbed until they uncovered the box. Nefrekeptah then cast the sand over the side of the boat until a sandbank formed, onto which the box was heaved.

The prince used his magic to subdue the snakes and scorpions, but his power had no effect on the enchanted serpent. He drew his sword and sliced off its head, but to his horror its head and body sprang together again; each time he repeated this, the same thing happened. By now, he realized he could only defeat the serpent by cunning, so he repeated the process, throwing sand on the parts he had severed, so that they could not join up.

He now turned his attention to the iron box, and opening each successive box, finally came to the Book of Thoth. Even as he read the first page of the book, the magic power, that he had dreamed of possessing for so long, flooded into his being.

When he showed the book to his wife, she also read the page, receiving power over the heavens and earth and an understanding of what animals were saying. On their way back to Memphis, however, a strange power seized hold of their son, dragging him down into the River Nile, but Nefrekeptah used a spell to save him, and the boy's body rose out of the water. But he could not bring his son back to life. He discovered that the great god Thoth was angry that the box had been taken and was using his own power to bring sorrow and punishment to the prince.

After burying their son, the couple headed for Memphis once again, but at the same point where their

FAR LEFT: Re-Harakhte, from the Great Temple at Abu Simbel.

PAGES 374–375: The banks of the Nile at Aswan.

Ptah on Setna's head. Setna leapt out of the ground, snatched the Book of Thoth, and fled.

His father advised Setna to return the Book of Thoth to the tomb, but Setna would not listen and spent hours on end poring over the book and studying its spells.

One day Setna saw a beautiful woman entering the Temple of Ptah. He discovered her name was Tabubua, and that she was the daughter of the high priest of the cat goddess Bastet. Setna instantly forgot everything, even the Book of Thoth, in his desire to marry her. But Setna was already married and Tabubua demanded he sacrificed his children to Bastet if he wished to marry her. This he did, and once his children were dead Tabubua seemed all the more desirable, that is, however, until she was transformed into a hideous, withered corpse.

Setna came abruptly to his senses and ran home to find his wife and children safe, finding it had only been a hideous dream. He realized that the dream had been a warning; now his only thought was to return the Book of Thoth as soon as possible.

He returned the book to the spirit of Nefrekeptah, and promised he would bring the bodies of Nefrekeptah's wife and child to rest alongside him in his tomb. After this had been done, Setna cast a spell on the tomb so that no one would be able to find the door. Later, a great sandstorm hid the tomb forever, and no one ever found the Book of Thoth again.

Many of the myths are great epics, and tell us much about Egyptian humour, customs and tastes. The story of the Princess of Bekhten was discovered in a large temple, built at Thebes during the reign of Ramesses III. It describes how the god of the moon,

Khonsu, the son of Amun and Mut, saved her life. Another story revolves around the sphinx and relates back to the time when Amenhotep was pharaoh of Egypt. It probably dates from around 1405 BC and recounts how the pharaoh's son, Tuthmose, promised the Great Sphinx of Giza a favour and became pharaoh in return.

There is an unfinished tale on the Harris Papyrus, now in the British Museum, that is believed to date from around the 18th dynasty. We do not know precisely how the papyrus was mutilated, though some believe it was partially eaten by a crocodile. It features a doomed prince, but the complete outcome of the tale is not known.

Some myths revolve around the quest for justice, such as the 12th-dynasty tale of the peasant and the workman. A fourth-dynasty myth, called the Golden Lotus, seems remarkably similar to the account in the Bible of the parting of the Red Sea by Moses, while the origins of the Cinderella story could well have lain in a story, written in the 26th dynasty, called the Girl with the Rose Red Slippers. There are also tales of shipwrecked sailors, the Trojan Wars, scorpions, the conception and birth of the great Queen Hatshepsut, which was found at her own temple at Deir-el-Bahri, while another story illustrates what it would have been like to visit Duat, the Land of the Dead.

Other tales revolve around court intrigues, such as the adventures of Sinuhe, a court official forced to go on the run when the pharaoh is assassinated. There are even tales that poke fun at the pharaohs, such as in the Tale of the Treasure Thief. In this, an individual is able to outwit Ramesses III, the story revealing the pharaoh as fallible while at the same time being just and fair. In

the end, the thief is allowed to marry a royal princess, when he continues to serve Ramesses III dutifully thereafter.

The myths, even though they were written onto papyrus and carved onto walls were, like the myths of other civilizations, designed to be passed down from generation to generation by word of mouth. We can see that some of the Egyptian myths are parables and fables, designed to teach the young the difference between right and wrong. They are enriched by the huge panoply of gods that appear in the stories, which, in turn, give a clue as to how they were created, many of the gods having been based possibly on early Egyptian rulers.

OPPOSITE: Mortuary temple of Hatshepsut, Deir el-Bahri.

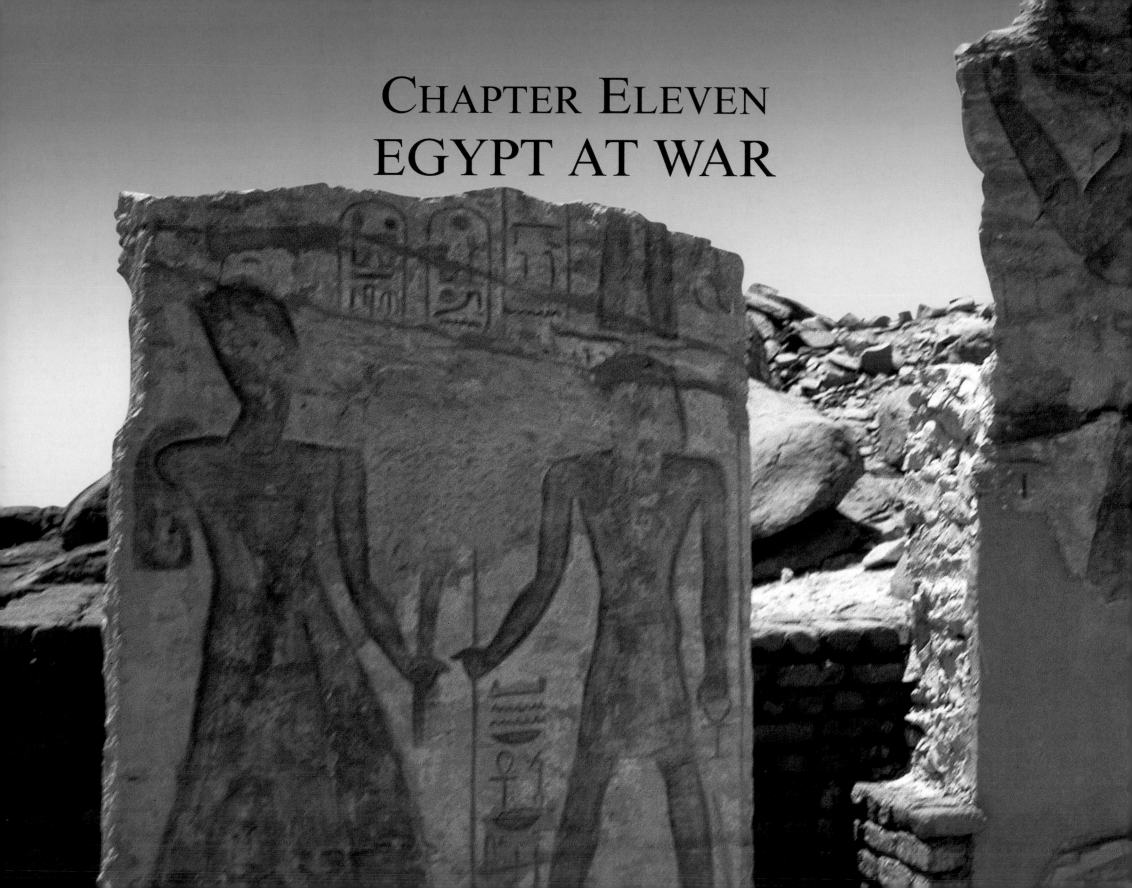

CHAPTER ELEVEN
EGYPT AT WAR

Egyptian chariots were certainly lighter and much faster than the types used in the Middle East. They had metal coverings on the axles and some of the wooden parts had metal sleeves, giving them added strength, even though the chariot itself would have been built from wood. The wooden parts were immersed in boiling water for several hours before being bent into shape. Ash was used for the axles and sycamore for the footboards, while wood bent into V-shapes made up the spokes of the wheels. Six pieces were used and these were glued together, so that each spoke became two halves of the V. The tips were fastened to the hub of the wheel by means of cattle intestines, which hardened as they dried out. The wheels themselves were made of sections of wood, tied to the framework by leather thongs. The two horses were yoked to the chassis via saddlebags on the horses' backs. Around their chests and bellies were leather girths and a single shaft was attached to the yoke to pull the chariot.

The driver held the reins, armed only with a whip, while the second man would have had a bow, slotted into a purpose-built sheath attached to the chariot's framework, with a similar receptacle on the other side of the chariot acting as a quiver for his arrows. Finally, he would have had a third receptacle

LEFT: The second pylon of Ramesses the Great at Luxor, with depictions of the Battle of Kadesh, fought between Ramesses II and the king of the Hittites.

RIGHT: Statue of Ramesses II, Luxor.

PAGES 386 & 387: The Ramesseum: view from the top of the temple.

containing several short throwing spears. The chariot, therefore, was built for speed and manoeuvrability and was able to pack a sizeable punch when used in large configurations on the battlefield.

As far as the Egyptians were concerned, however, the chariot was never uppermost in the organization of the army, merely a supporting arm, its purpose being to protect the Egyptian infantry from heavier enemy chariots. Compared with the Egyptian chariot, the Hittite version was very much heavier; it had a crew of three, and was designed to charge the enemy infantry, using the weight of the chariot itself to break through the line. This is what happened to the Egyptian army at the Battle of Kadesh, and it was a good tactic, provided that the battle was being fought on open terrain. The Hittite chariot was extremely unstable in rough conditions, while the Egyptian chariot, on the other hand, was intentionally lighter, being more suited to the Egyptian terrain.

Egyptian chariots attacked the enemy chariots in a well-spaced line, enabling them to wheel around rapidly, once the enemy chariots had been penetrated. As the chariots charged forward, the second passenger would open fire with his bow, switching to short throwing spears at closer range. While the chariots were not designed for impact, hand-to-hand combat was

OPPOSITE: The seventh pylon of Tuthmose III, decorated with victory scenes and the names of defeated enemies, Karnak.

LEFT: Mahes, Lord of the Massacre, in the shape of a lion savaging a prisoner. National Museum, Khartoum.

common, when the passenger would resort to a thrusting spear or sword.

Running alongside the Egyptian chariots were armed men bearing spears and bows. Their job was to kill or capture the enemy crew, once the line had been broken. With the Egyptian chariots behind them, and the chariot runners closing in on them from the front, the enemy chariots were at the mercy of the Egyptian troops. Chariots were also useful for pursuing routed enemy troops, able to catch them up, overtake them, then capture the slower-moving chariots.

Also central to the army were the troops known as the Braves of the King. These were the infantry that spearheaded attacks on the battlefield. By the 18th dynasty, another group had emerged; these were mostly royal bodyguards known as the Retainers.

As already mentioned, the Egyptian army of the New Kingdom period relied heavily on mercenaries, and Libyan, Sherden and Medjay forces all served among the ranks, with some attaining positions of importance; by the 19th dynasty, mercenaries were even being deployed against their own former tribes. Indeed, mercenary commanders became so established in the Egyptian army that the rulers of the 22nd and 23rd dynasties of Egypt were the actual descendants of Libyan mercenaries.

The tactics used by the Egyptians were not very sophisticated. In cases where there were sieges, the Egyptian army would simply surround the city or fortress and wait until the enemy was starving to death. Sometimes the Egyptians would inform their enemies when they were about to begin battle and if the enemy was not ready the battle would be postponed. This sometimes caused problems for the Egyptians when they were attacked unawares.

After a successful battle, the loot was initially turned over to the pharaoh, some of which was then given to the temple priests and the rest to deserving soldiers. Sometimes, literally thousands of weapons, chariots and horses were captured and brought back with some pride to Egypt, while enemy soldiers and civilians were either taken prisoner or destined to become slaves. If vanquished enemy princes accepted the pharaoh as their overlord, then they were allowed to keep their lands.

The Egyptians had been happy for generations to use weapons that many would have regarded as archaic. Therefore it was not unusual to see Egyptian soldiers with stone weapons fighting alongside others bearing more sophisticated metal arms. Before the introduction of the bow, the only alternative had been the throwing stick, but during the Old and Middle Kingdoms, longer-range weapons came into use, including slings and bows. For hand-to-hand combat, the infantry used an assortment of clubs, axes, maces, daggers and spears, many of which would have had a simple wooden handle and a sharp edge made of either stone or hammered copper. Arrows were made from reeds and were given bronze heads; indeed, Egyptian bronze weapons continued to be used well into the Iron Age period. A major reason for this, perhaps, is that Egypt had no iron deposits of its own, which was a key factor that allowed the Assyrians, with their iron weapons, to conquer Egypt.

Initially, the Egyptians used shields made from turtle shells, but later they protected themselves with rectangular wooden shields, covered in leather.

The New Kingdom period saw some improvements in weaponry and the introduction of a sickle sword, called the *khepesh*, while body armour was also introduced. Egyptian soldiers had previously worn leather triangular aprons over short kilts, but now coats of chain mail were coming into use. Initially, only the king wore this new armour, but by the 19th dynasty infantry was being issued with leather or cloth tunics covered in metal scales. Helmets were not in general use before the Late Period, although Sherden mercenaries had been wearing them for some time.

The Egyptian navy was seen primarily as a supporting arm of the army. Occasionally it was engaged in battle, but sailors effectively operated as soldiers at sea. Many of the ships were built at Byblos in Phoenicia, but a naval base was set up close to Memphis and was of particular importance during the 18th dynasty. Tuthmose III used his navy to take the coastal cities of Phoenicia, leapfrogging from one harbour to the next as his ground forces advanced.

The organization of the naval forces was not dissimilar to that of the army. On paper, the pharaoh was the commander-in-chief, but a prince usually assumed the role in practice. Admirals were assigned to distinct naval formations and a chief of ship's captains was directly responsible to one of the admirals and would command what was basically a squadron. A captain's mate supported the ship's captain and a commander-of-troops was assigned to each ship to take charge of the infantry or marines onboard.

OPPOSITE: Mural of a battle, from the temple of Ramesses III at Medinet Habu.

Another individual was responsible for controlling the rowers and, finally, there were the sailors themselves; these endured the worst physical conditions of all on board the ship.

The Egyptians had a police force, which was not directly linked to the army itself. It was responsible for maintaining order and was considered to be the guardian and protector of the Egyptian population, dealing with thefts, troublemakers and tax evaders; it was also the job of the police to expel nomads and hunt for escaped prisoners. The force used trained dogs to patrol the desert frontiers and meted out summary punishments to those who broke the law.

Once Egypt had expanded beyond its natural boundaries, fortifications were needed to protect the newly acquired lands. These were tall, thick-walled fortresses, usually built on hills, and mostly constructed from mud brick. They were used to accommodate garrisons of troops and also acted as surveillance posts.

During the Middle Kingdom, fortresses were reinforced with wooden beams, an interesting development being a wall that changed its angle halfway up, thus preventing the use of scaling ladders. Whenever the Egyptians came across foreign fortresses, they promptly copied them. Some of them, therefore, had parapets, ramps and ditches, while others were made of stone and had battlements, turrets, keeps and moats.

Rocky outcrops in the Sinai Desert.

Over the period of Ancient Egypt, its various enemies belonged to two categories; first came the empires that possessed resources needed by the Egyptians, which included the Mitanni and the Hatti. The second were those who were threatening to invade Egypt, and which included the Libyans and the Sea Peoples.

To the south of Egypt lay Nubia. The Egyptians reviled the Nubians, but had been making incursions into their country for generations in order to steal Nubia's resources, including prisoners-of-war, who would eventually be used as slaves. Cattle were also highly sought, as were more exotic resources, such as ebony, ivory and ostrich feathers, while parts of Nubia were permanently settled by the Egyptians because they were rich in gold. By the New Kingdom period, Nubia had effectively become a province of Egypt; such was the assimilation that had occurred between the two countries that, for a short period at least, Nubian pharaohs came to power in Egypt.

The Egyptians referred to the Libyans as the Tjehenu or Tjemehu, and they are shown on Egyptian wall decorations as a bearded, dark-skinned people, though some had blue eyes and fair hair. In fact, they were not a single race and the territory they occupied lay to the north-west of the Nile valley. During the New Kingdom period, the pharaohs Merenptah and Ramesses III fought major campaigns to prevent Libyan invasions, there being numerous reliefs showing them slaughtering Libyan chiefs. On occasions, when the Libyans were proving troublesome, the Egyptians would launch punitive campaigns, aimed at creating havoc and capturing prisoners. Over the generations, captured Libyans were settled in military colonies and

became known as the Meshwesh and, for a short period during the 22nd dynasty, were even in control of Egypt itself.

The word Hyksos is somewhat confusing, in that it meant 'ruler of foreign lands', as far as the Egyptians were concerned. The Hyksos were Asiatic semi-nomads, who arrived after the Middle Kingdom period as invaders, armed with copper weapons, chariots and horses. Eventually, Pharaoh Ahmose I, the founder of the New Kingdom period, was able to expel them from Egypt, signalling a period when Egypt was no longer content to defend its own borders, but would sue for war in Syria and Palestine. This led to direct clashes between the pharaohs of the New Kingdom and the Mitanni, and ultimately with the Hatti and Assyria.

The stretch of the Mediterranean coast to the north of the Sinai Desert, specifically Canaan, was regarded as a vital buffer zone by the Egyptians, but taking it and holding it had never been an easy task. The Mitanni and the Hittites had long used the area as a launching pad from which to attack Egypt, while Syria itself, where the Mitanni people lived, was at the very hub of world trade. Goods flowed into Syria from the Near East and from the Aegean and it was also an area that had good natural resources. Consequently, it was destined to become the focus of power struggles in the Middle East for hundreds of years.

The Hittites inhabited parts of modern-day Turkey and northern Syria. Under their strong ruler, Labarna, the empire had grown significantly, and it was now beginning to make inroads into Mesopotamia. The Hittite empire began to weaken in around 1500 BC, just as the Mitanni was gaining power in northern Syria and Mesopotamia. A struggle would develop between Mitanni and Egypt for control of Syria, but meanwhile the Hittites had far from disappeared. They rose again in around 1400 BC and within 200 years had become one of the most powerful kingdoms in the world, having displaced thousands of people in the course of their great expansion. Egypt now had the task of facing the Hittites in Syria.

Hittite military power was centred on the chariot and infantry, and the Hittites may well have worn uniforms and had helmets and bronze-scale armour. They were reputed to be good strategists and were certainly wily enemies. It was only a matter of time before the Hittites and the Egyptians engaged in a major campaign, that would determine the future of both empires.

Among those routed from their lands by the Hittites were the Sea Peoples or the Peoples of the Sea – a loose confederation of different tribes. They had been driven out not only by military expansion but also by crop failure and famine, and this had sent them looking for more fertile lands. They had already made incursions into the Aegean, and had arrived on Egypt's delta coast, where they joined with the Libyan tribes in creating a force of some 16,000 men.

Soon, they began to move south towards Memphis and the Pharaoh Merenptah, but they could not be allowed to take the city. In a six-hour battle, 6,000 of the Sea Peoples were killed and many others were captured and settled in military colonies. This was   not to be the end of the story, however; they remained strong, destined to be instrumental in destroying the Hittite empire.

It was not until the reign of Ramesses III that they returned to attack Egypt, even though the Egyptians had by now fortified their borders. Once again the Egyptians slaughtered the Sea Peoples and Ramesses III's victory was immortalized forever on the walls of his mortuary temple.

The Battle of Kadesh, which has already been mentioned, is remarkably well recorded. It was a battle between the Egyptians, under Ramesses II, and the Hittites and their allies, under Muwatallish, in which the control of Syria would be determined. As already seen, the great powers of the Middle East knew full well that Syria was an important crossroads; its control was also of vital importance because it was at the centre of world trade.

The Egyptians had been fighting for control of the region for some time, but by the New Kingdom period the pharaohs had come to the conclusion that control of Syria was vital to the consolidation of their empire. Egypt had been struggling with the Mitanni and Hatti for years, which had led, during the reign of Tuthmose III, to the Battle of Megiddo, a fortress that controlled the main road north to Lebanon and east to the Euphrates river. The Egyptians, having had no major battle for 20 years, approached Megiddo to find the enemy waiting for them. It was also the pharaoh's first taste of combat.

Opposing the Egyptians were troops gathered under no less than 330 kings. The enemy forces deployed outside the fortress and launched the first attack. It was routed, and the Egyptians gave chase, but instead of overrunning the fortress, the enemy began to loot the abandoned camps, when the chance of storming the fortress was lost; the city did not fall for

some time, and only after there had been an extremely lengthy siege.

The pharaoh's subsequent victory and capture of the city left the Egyptians with the impression that southern Syria was a part of Egypt. Peace treaties were subsequently signed, but the revival of the Hittite empire now threatened bloodshed as before. The Egyptians could not have predicted how war would come, but a small kingdom, called Amurru, nominally under the control of the Egyptians, occupied a key position in Syria. The ruler of this kingdom began to expand at the expense of some of the smaller states in the region, and despite complaints from the Pharaoh Amenhotep III, nothing more was done. Mitanni was more inclined to act, but by then the new Hittite king, Suppiluliumas, had begun to capture Mitanni-held northern Syria.

The Hittite army crossed the Euphrates and swept aside what was left of the Mitanni empire, capturing the strategically important city of Kadesh. The Egyptians were slow to appreciate the importance of this; the Hittites had large numbers of troops in Syria, and very few Egyptian troops stood in their way.

When Seti I came to power, he was bent on retrieving Egypt's position in Syria. He led an army into the region, creating a precedent for future pharaohs. Seti I is said to have captured Kadesh and defeated a Hittite army in northern Syria, but the Hittites recaptured Kadesh, or possibly had the city returned to them as the result of a promise of peace. This situation, however, was far from acceptable to Ramesses II, Seti I's successor.

The Red Sea.and the Sinai Peninsula.

By this stage, the Amurru kingdom, having once been Egyptian, allied itself with the Hittites, who decided to return to Egypt again. This only added to the confusion and the new Hittite king, Muwatallish, knew he would have to defend Syria from a determined Egyptian attack.

Ramesses II approached Kadesh at the head of the lead corps of the Egyptian army and crossed the River Orontes to approach the city from the south. Here, he encountered Bedouin tribesmen, from whom he learned that the Hittite army lay actually to the north. It appears, however, that they were lying, being in the pay of the Hittite king. Ramesses seems to have believed them, however, ordering his troops to press on and make camp to the north-west of Kadesh.

Eventually, he learned the truth from captured enemy scouts: the Hittite army was not to the north, but was encamped behind Kadesh and was preparing itself for battle. Ramesses II was very exposed, in that he had only his own corps with him; he sent a division of his troops back to hurry the others forward, but the division was ambushed by 2,500 Hittite chariots as it crossed the Plain of Kadesh.

The Hittite force wheeled round to the north and attacked Ramesses II's camp, overrunning it. With his troops fleeing from the enemy force, Ramesses donned his armour and jumped into his chariot, seeking to hold off the enemy attack. By now the Hittite chariot force was floundering and they launched a further 1,000 more, but just as they were about to crash into Ramesses II's men, Egyptian reinforcements arrived. The Egyptians were able to hold off the Hittites, who eventually pulled back, having suffered huge casualties.

This version of events is purely Egyptian and in the absence of any other real evidence, we cannot know how much of it is true. What we do know is that a peace treaty was signed after the battle, which not only fixed the borders between the two nations, but also committed the Hittites and the Egyptians to support one another if attacked by a third party. Thus Ramesses II made peace with his arch-enemies, which ended the war in Syria. The treaty was cemented some years later, when Ramesses married the daughter of the Hittite king. Peace continued throughout Ramesses II's reign, and continued until the Hittite empire finally fell.

Much of the information and reliefs, that still exist, feature the kings and princes of Egypt, but it was the rank and file of the Egyptian army which bore the brunt. During the New Kingdom, new recruits faced an incredibly tough time when they were first conscripted; they would have been required to carry out physical exercise and train to use weapons wearing only a short kilt and a feather in their hair. They were beaten for the smallest breach of discipline, but on the other hand, could be rewarded if the army performed well, when they could expect trophies, slave girls and

OPPOSITE: Set and Horus blessing Ramesses II, from the Great Temple of Re-Harakhte, Abu Simbel.

PAGE 398: The Ramesseum, the mortuary temple of Ramesses II, Luxor.

PAGE 399: A hand fallen from a statue of Ramesses II, Luxor.

possibly grants of land. Soldiers were presented with the equivalent of medals: some were awarded necklaces of golden bees, while others would be given golden bracelets or would receive the honorific Amkhu, which entitled them to be buried at the pharaoh's expense.

As we have seen, clubs were the earliest weapons used by the Egyptians, and they were generally made of wood, absorbing the shock of impact quite efficiently. The logical development was the mace, essentially a lump of stone on a wooden club, which would have been used throughout the whole of the Ancient Egyptian period. Some of the stone mace heads were extremely well-crafted, though they were not much use against a man clad in armour and with a helmet on his head, when they would often shatter. Various different shapes were tried before stone was eventually set aside and replaced by copper. We often see reliefs of pharaohs symbolically striking an enemy with a mace, but in truth it was no longer a particularly useful weapon of war.

The practical solution was to replace the mace with an edged weapon and the Egyptians did not have to look very far, in that they regularly used axes for peaceful purposes, which could be adapted for war. The infantry was accordingly armed with battleaxes, which were not particularly effective against scaled body armour. As a result, we see two different types of Egyptian axe emerging: one armed with a cutting edge, the other being a piercing weapon. The cutting weapon was effective against an enemy without armour or helmets, whereas the piercing axe was designed to penetrate them both, though it did not make an appearance until the Middle Kingdom period. Variants of these had been used during the Old and Middle

Kingdoms, some of which had long shafts, while others were scalloped. By the New Kingdom period the Egyptians were producing very long, narrow axeheads, able to penetrate enemy armour, and by the end of the period, the sword was replacing the axe as the most practical close-quarter weapon of war. However, Egyptian soldiers tended to carry on using flint knives, maces and battleaxes, long after they ceased to be of any practical use in combat.

Swords and daggers were originally reserved for ceremonial purposes, daggers, in any case, being ineffective against men armed with maces or battleaxes. Once metal had become more readily available, longer-edged weapons could be produced; the swords had long, cutting edges and often had either wooden or ivory handles. A good sharp edge could not be produced on copper, but bronze was perfect for making swords. It could be given its basic shape before being heated, hammered and cooled to give it a keen edge.

The Egyptians probably learned about swords from the Sea Peoples, who used straight two-edged blades with sharp points, as opposed to the Egyptian curved weapon. Above all, the Sea Peoples' weapons were made from iron, which was far less brittle than the Egyptian bronze. In the army of Ramesses III, Egyptian troops were armed with curved cutting swords, while the mercenaries had pointed piercing swords. Scabbards were not used, but an eye was fixed to the sword so that it could be fastened to a belt.

Ancient Egyptian projectile weapons went through a similar evolution. The throwing stick was still in use towards the end of the New Kingdom period, but during the Old and Middle Kingdoms, spears with copper or flint blades were being deployed by the

infantry. The spear had good penetrative powers if thrown or thrust at the enemy, but the blade, being larger, was more expensive to produce than the smaller arrowheads. It is also possible that forked bronze spears were used, and examples of such weapons, resembling pitchforks, have been excavated. Most of the spears used by the Ancient Egyptians were no longer than a man's height, being in effect javelins rather than thrusting spears.

But it was the bow-and-arrow that was Egypt's most useful weapon. Initially, they were made from pairs of antelope horns, joined together by a central wooden piece. Early arrows had three feathers and were of either sharpened hardwood or tipped with flint; bronze points came somewhat later. During the New Kingdom, the newer composite bow was imported into Egypt. These could be made into more powerful weapons by adding horn to the belly of a wooden bow and using compressed sinew to produce greater tension, making it penetrative enough to pierce even scaled armour.

Slings were probably used, but quickly perished, being made from animal skin or cloth. Only the slingshots themselves have survived, most of them pebbles, although lead sling bullets were used later on.

The Egyptian shield certainly dates from the Predynastic Period, but body armour and helmets did not appear until much later. Shields were usually up to 5ft (1.5m) in height, with a tapered top, and were made from cowhide stretched over a wooden frame. By the New Kingdom period, bronze was being used for shields, though the protection afforded was not much better. The round shield never really became popular, even though hundreds of them had been

captured from the Sea Peoples during the reign of Ramesses III.

As mentioned, helmets came in very late, although mercenaries had been wearing them for some years. They seem to have been fairly basic affairs, worn in the main by senior military commanders or officers.

Armour was not popular because it was hot, heavy and restricted movement. Most Egyptians went into battle wearing a belt and a triangular loincloth and some wore the short linen kilt; occasionally they are depicted with a band of webbing across their shoulders and chest. Even if they had wanted to wear armour, most soldiers would have found it too expensive. Armour was sometimes worn purely for ostentation and to show how rich and powerful an individual presumed himself to be.

With the exception of certain periods in Egypt's history, the Egyptians were largely defensive, but once they realized that expansion would ultimately protect them from invasion, they took to such adventures readily and vigorously. The Egyptian army was neither a particularly flexible nor effective force, but it invariably more than held its own against similarly armed and equally aggressive foes. These, however, did not have the same advantage, in that Egypt was being led by a warrior god.

FAR LEFT: Neith, a goddess of war and funerals, from the tomb of Nefertari at Abu Simbel.

RIGHT: The feet of the fallen statue of Ramesses II in the Ramesseum, Luxor.

CHAPTER TWELVE
THE END OF THE PHARAOHS

CHAPTER TWELVE
THE END OF THE PHARAOHS

Nectanebo I was the founder of the 30th dynasty, which saw the last of the native-born rulers of Egypt. Nectanebo was probably a descendant of Nepherites I, the first ruler of the 29th dynasty, and was responsible for bringing that dynasty to an end. Nectanebo came to power in around 380 BC, having been the general of one of the last rulers of the 29th dynasty, Nepherites II, and having suppressed a revolt staged by Hakoris, his pharaoh's predecessor. He eventually turned on his royal masters and an Athenian general, named Khabrias, was probably instrumental in bringing him to power. Nectanebo I possibly married Khabrias's daughter. He was also married to Udjashu, who would provide him with Teos, his son and heir.

At the beginning of Nectanebo's rule, the Persian king, Artaxerxes II, whose dynasty had once ruled in Egypt, sent a combined Persian and Greek force to invade Egypt and return it to the Persian fold. Luckily for Nectanebo, the allies did not trust one another and held back from storming Memphis: the Persians, under Pharnabazes, decided to wait until Persian reinforcements arrived, while the Greeks, under Iphicrates, wanted to attack Memphis immediately. The delay gave Nectanebo the chance to launch a counter-attack, which forced the invaders out of Egypt.

Before his death, Nectanebo I established Teos, his son, as his co-regent. Teos, coming to power in 365 BC, decided to deal with the Persian threat by taking the offensive, enlisting the aid of Greek mercenaries and launching an ill-fated expedition. His generals and the Egyptian troops abandoned him, however, and the Greeks subsequently deserted. He was captured by the Persians and lived in exile until his death.

In the aftermath of this failed offensive, Nectanebo II was able to usurp the throne in 360 BC. He was the brother of Teos, whose preparations for war and heavy taxation had precipitated Egypt into revolt. Nectanebo II took advantage of the situation and would rule for 18 years, leaving the Persians to squabble over the succession. By 350 BC, however, Artaxerxes III had gained control of the Persian empire and was ready to move against Egypt once more.

A Spartan, Lamias, and an Athenian called Diophatens, commanded the Egyptian forces facing this new invasion. But the Persians were decisively beaten back and Artaxerxes III began to gather a much larger army in Babylon, having moved his navy to Sidon. Nectanebo II promised the king of Sidon he would come to his aid if he rebelled against the Persians. The king agreed and Nectanebo II despatched 4,000 Greek mercenaries to assist the king, led by Mentor, a Greek general from the island of Rhodes.

The Persians were held back only for a short time, because by the autumn of 343 BC, the Persians were back and storming into northern Egypt. Nectanebo II mustered an army of some 100,000 men, including 20,000 Greeks. They waited for the Persians to close on them at Pelusium, in the eastern delta region, but the Egyptians were outflanked and were forced to fall back, forcing Nectanebo II to abandon Memphis and retreat into southern Egypt. For a short time he was able to hold the Persians back, but was eventually forced further south into Nubia. This time the Persians were here to stay and the 31st dynasty, which would have three rulers, ushered in the second period of Persian domination in Egypt.

Artaxerxes III effectively became the new pharaoh of Egypt, but he was murdered by one of his commanders in the summer of 338 BC, having ruled for six years. The same commander, Bagoas, would also be

Kiosk of Qertassi, Kalabsha, Aswan.

the murderer of Artaxerxes III's son, Arses, who died in 336 BC.

Darius III was the last Persian Achemenid emperor and the effective pharaoh of Egypt from 335–332 BC. But he was destined to face Alexander the Great, suffering a shattering defeat at the Battle of Gaugamela. In the aftermath, he was murdered by one of his own generals, Bessus, which effectively ended the Persian domination of Egypt and heralded in the longer-lasting Greco-Roman period.

Alexander the Great was welcomed by the people when he rode in triumph into Egypt in 332 BC. The Persians had oppressed the Egyptians and Alexander seemed to be very different from the Greeks encountered by the Egyptians in the past. He was ready to embrace the Egyptian religion and culture and when he visited the Oracle of Amun at Siwa, declared 'the son of Amun'. From that point on, he was viewed by the Egyptians in a similar light as the pharaohs of the golden age. Alexander left Egypt in 331 BC, leaving Cleomenes in control.

After the untimely death of Alexander in Babylon, his generals, even though they had inherited specific portions of the new empire to control, began to squabble among themselves, and it was ultimately Ptolemy I Soter who took control of Egypt. He had been a childhood friend of Alexander, one of his royal bodyguards, and a trusted military commander.

The 30th-dynasty tomb of Umm al-Ubeyda, Siwa.

As the new Ptolemaic dynasty dawned, so Alexander's empire began to fragment. The supposed successor to Alexander the Great had been Perdiccas, who marched on Ptolemy in the spring of 321 BC. His army was repulsed close to Memphis and Perdiccas was murdered, but it failed to resolve the disputes between Alexander's heirs, who were known collectively as the Diadochi, or successors.

The most powerful of these was Antigonus Gonatus, whose rivals were Ptolemy of Egypt, Cassander of Macedon and Lysimachus, who controlled Thrace and parts of Asia Minor. Antigonus marched against Cassander, and Ptolemy attacked Antigonus's son, Demetrius, in retaliation, defeating him at Gaza in 312 BC.

But the squabbles continued and Ptolemy lost a sea battle against Demetrius, fought off Cyprus in 306 BC. When Rhodes was defended in 305 BC, there was more fighting, until the battle of Ipsus in 301 BC, when Antigonus was finally killed; the three allies were then able to split Antigonus's empire between them, with Ptolemy also acquiring Palestine and Lower Syria.

To cement his relationship with the Egyptian people, Ptolemy adopted the name Meryamun Setepenre, meaning 'beloved of Amun, chosen of Re'. He may have married a daughter of Nectanebo II, but his favourite wife was Eurydice, who was the daughter of the regent of Macedon, Antipater, and with whom Ptolemy had at least four children.

Ptolemy I ruled until 285 or 283 BC, his major construction being the Pharos (Lighthouse) of Alexandria. He also created the Great Library of Alexandria, once the largest of its kind in the world. It was during his rule that the Hebrew Bible was possibly

translated into Greek. In the latter stages of his reign he shared the co-regency with one of his sons, who became Ptolemy II. No one knows where Ptolemy I was buried, but it was possibly at Alexandria.

Ptolemy II's rule was also successful and there was continued expansion. He aimed to gain control over the Aegean, the eastern Mediterranean and the Black Sea; allied with anti-Macedonian factions, he vied with Macedon for control over the region. At home, Egypt's new capital, Alexandria, had also expanded and grown rich, becoming an important centre of study. Ptolemy II completed his father's great works in the city and at some point married his full sister, having already married the daughter of Lysimachus. Ptolemy III, the son of his first wife, succeeded him.

Ptolemy III adopted the improbable Egyptian name of Iwaennetjerwysenwy Sekhemankhre Setepamun, which means 'heir of the beneficent gods, chosen of Ptah, powerful is the son of Re, living image of Amun'. Ptolemy II had made peace with Antiochus II and had offered his daughter as part of the deal. Antiochus II was already married to Laodice, but to seal their treaty he left Laodice and married Ptolemy's daughter, Berenice. By 246 BC, however, Antiochus had left Berenice and her infant son in Antioch to live again with Laodice in Asia Minor.

Laodice eventually poisoned Berenice, Berenice's infant son, and in time, Antiochus himself, proclaiming her own son Seleucus II Callinicus king. There were other sons in the mix and some of them had already met with unfortunate ends. Laodice also had Ptolemy III's sister and her son killed, and the Egyptian ruler sacked Antioch in revenge, occupying Antioch for two years until 244 BC.

Ptolemy III continued to support anti-Macedonian forces, but distanced himself militarily from the squabbles in mainland Greece. He organized the building of the Great Temple to Horus at Edfu, along with several structures at Karnak. He ruled for 25 years and was probably buried in Alexandria. He was succeeded by his son, Ptolemy IV, in 222 BC.

Ptolemy IV was nothing like his predecessors and the new king of Syria, Antiochus III, decided to take advantage of his weakness, capturing portions of Phoenicia, even though he was no great military leader himself. Nevertheless, a major conflict was certainly inevitable and in the summer of 217 BC. Ptolemy IV, at the head of 55,000 men, including elephants from Somalia, took to the field against Antiochus III's army of 68,000 men, clashing at Raphia in Palestine. Antiochus III had even larger elephants stationed at intervals along his front. To begin with, Ptolemy was fearful of these larger creatures, but Antiochus III over-extended himself and was defeated, after a pitch battle had been fought.

After trying to settle the border disputes, Ptolemy IV returned to Egypt and married his sister, who would provide him with an heir. During his reign, Ptolemy IV allowed native Egyptian troops to establish an independent country in the south, which for a time was ruled by native pharaohs. Ptolemy IV is credited with

LEFT: The hypostyle hall of the temple at Deir el-Medina, begun by Ptolemy IV.

OPPOSITE: The Oracle of Amun at Siwa.

building temples at Tanis, Thebes, Karnak and with the completion of the Temple of Horus at Edfu. He died in the summer of 204 BC and was succeeded by Ptolemy V, his son, who became pharaoh in name only, being only five years old. True power lay in the hands of two of Ptolemy IV's advisors, Sosibius and Agathocles.

Sosibius and Agathocles had murdered Ptolemy V's mother and the wife of Ptolemy IV, but when this was discovered, Agathocles was lynched and Sosibius was made to disappear. A succession of advisors took control of Egypt until Ptolemy V was able to rule in his own name.

Syria, a long-term enemy, was still a major concern, now ruled by the Seleucid dynasty, whose vast empire stretched from Asia Minor through to Mesopotamia and Syria. A secret pact had been made between the Seleucid ruler, Antiochus, and Philip V of Macedon, whereby they would attack Egypt and share the empire between them. Thus began the fifth Syrian War.

It went well for the allies and Palestine was lost, including the important port of Sidon. But Ptolemy V had been crowned king in Memphis in 197 BC, and it was time for him to ensure that no more of Egypt's empire went to the enemy. He entered into an uneasy peace with the Seleucids in 192 BC, when he married the daughter of Antiochus the Great. Her name was

LEFT: The Temple of Horus at Edfu.

RIGHT: Hathor wearing the solar disk between cow horns. Temple of Ptolemy IV at Deir el-Medina.

Cleopatra and she would produce two sons and a daughter, all of whom would eventually rule Egypt. Ptolemy V died, probably of poisoning, at the age of 28 in 181 BC. Fortunately, he had been able to crush the revolt in southern Egypt ten years earlier, and had reunited the country.

Ptolemy VI was still young when he succeeded his father, so Egypt was left in the hands of Cleopatra I, the daughter of Antiochus the Great, for the first five years. After five years, however, Cleopatra I died and officials appointed themselves guardians.

Stupidly, the guardians, Eulaeus and Lenaeus, declared war on Antiochus IV in 170 BC, which sparked the sixth Syrian War. It was the same year that Ptolemy VI declared himself fit to rule. He married his sister, Cleopatra II, and appointed his younger brother, Ptolemy VIII, as his co-regent.

Antiochus IV was only too willing to take advantage of the situation and headed south in the spring of 169 BC, destroying the first Egyptian army he encountered. Next, he probably captured Ptolemy VI, taking control of virtually the whole of Egypt, with the exception of Alexandria. Ptolemy VI had not relinquished hope of ruling Egypt, but the Egyptians wanted nothing to do with him and decided to proclaim Ptolemy VIII joint ruler with his sister, Cleopatra II. Since Ptolemy VI was under the control of Antiochus, the Seleucid was happy to side with the original ruler, but in reality both Ptolemys now ruled Egypt, Ptolemy VI, by virtue of Antiochus IV's support, and Ptolemy VIII by the will of the people.

The two Ptolemys and Cleopatra decided to ask for the assistance of Rome, which was unable to help directly; this was because Rome was already fighting

Perseus in mainland Greece; instead, Rome sent three members of the Senate to negotiate the peace between Egypt and the Seleucids, who decreed that Antiochus should vacate both Egypt and Cyprus.

Antiochus wanted time to consider, but the leader of the Senate mission, Caius Popilius Laenas, simply drew a circle in the sand around his feet, telling Antiochus he must answer before he would be allowed to leave the circle. Antiochus saw nothing for it but to comply; for a short time, the brothers and their sister continued to rule Egypt.

With three rulers in Egypt, the situation could not last, and in May 163 BC, the brothers agreed to partition the Ptolemaic empire. Ptolemy VI took Egypt, and his brother settled for the province of Cyrenaica, while Ptolemy VIII also wanted Cyprus, a claim backed by the Romans. Ptolemy VI then tried to have his brother assassinated, which must have been a close call, because he had the scars to show the Romans when he went to them to press his claim. He headed back for Cyprus, which he tried to capture with token Roman military support, but his brother captured him instead. Rather than killing Ptolemy VIII, however, Ptolemy VI offered his own daughter, Cleopatra Thea, to his brother in marriage, before packing him off back to Cyrenaica.

Just as things were beginning to settle down again, an individual called Balas appeared on the scene, claiming to be the son of Antiochus IV. Balas was backed by Rome and also covertly by Ptolemy VI, who offered his daughter, Cleopatra Thea, to Balas, her marriage to his brother having since failed.

By this time, the ruler of the Seleucids was Demetrius II, who decided to march into Syria to expel

Balas. Ptolemy VI marched north, claiming he was defending his son-in-law. Ptolemy pressed on towards Antioch and to his amazement, its citizens proclaimed him their new king. Ptolemy was now in a difficult position: he knew Rome would not approve of this development and persuaded Antioch to keep Demetrius II. He proclaimed the marriage between his daughter and Balas void and married her off to Demetrius II instead. It is probable that while this was happening, Balas tried to have Ptolemy VI assassinated, so Ptolemy was not displeased when an Arab chieftain presented him with Balas's head. Ptolemy VI died in 145 BC, leaving the widowed Cleopatra in Alexandria to care for his young heir, Ptolemy VII.

Ptolemy VII would have been around 16 when he came to the throne, but he was forced to face his father's brother, Ptolemy VIII, who had strong support in Egypt. But the real power lay with Cleopatra II, Ptolemy VII's mother, and Ptolemy VIII accordingly married her. The young Ptolemy VII was killed during the wedding feast.

Ptolemy VIII's eye soon fell on the daughter of Cleopatra II, his niece and stepdaughter. For many, it was an intolerable situation, in that he now had two children with Cleopatra III and a son by Cleopatra II. Ptolemy VIII was forced out of Alexandria and fled to Cyprus, where he plotted his return to Egypt, leaving Cleopatra II to reign in his place.

Temple of Ptolemy IV, Deir el-Medina.

She too had problems: an individual called Harsiese, possibly the last native Egyptian to hold the title of pharaoh, led a revolt in Thebes. Cleopatra II quickly dealt with him, but by 129 BC, Ptolemy VIII was ready to invade Egypt. In desperation, Cleopatra II offered the throne of Egypt to Demetrius II, and the Seleucid began to head south to claim the throne. Meanwhile, Cleopatra headed north to seek the protection of her daughter, Cleopatra Thea, while Ptolemy VIII's troops seized control of the country. Alexandria held out for a year or so, until around 126 BC, and when it fell, Ptolemy took bloody revenge on the city.

Now back in control of Egypt, Ptolemy VIII ruled until 116 BC. He outlived Cleopatra II and willed Egypt to his daughter and wife, Cleopatra III, together with either of her sons with whom she preferred to rule.

There were two sons: Lathyros, whom Cleopatra hated, and Alexander, whom she loved. Lathyros was already the governor of Cyprus and was favoured by the people of Egypt. Lathyros was married to his sister, Cleopatra IV, but at the insistence of his mother they were divorced and he was forced to marry Cleopatra Selene, one of his other sisters. Cleopatra IV, meanwhile, headed for Cyprus, where she attempted to raise troops, determined to marry Ptolemy Alexander, Lathyros's brother. He refused to marry her, so she headed instead for Syria, and using her army as a dowry, married Antiochus IX, who was the son of Cleopatra Thea. In 107 BC, Lathyros tried to murder his mother, Cleopatra III, but the attempt failed and he was forced to flee.

After Lathyros had been driven out of Egypt, Cleopatra III at last had her own way and co-ruled

Egypt with her son, Alexander; but she soon grew tired of this arrangement and forced him to leave Alexandria. He returned some time later, making overtures towards a reconciliation, but had her assassinated instead.

Alexander would later die in a naval battle and Lathyros did not return to Egypt until he was in his 50s. He tried to pick up the pieces of the Ptolemaic empire, but died in his early 60s. His left no legitimate heir to the throne, his sons having died before him, and only a daughter, Cleopatra Berenice, was left.

Cleopatra Berenice had been married to Alexander, but after Alexander died, she was obliged to marry her younger son or stepson, Ptolemy XI. Only 19 days after the wedding, however, he murdered her. Ptolemy XI, or more precisely Ptolemy XI Alexander II, was Ptolemy X's son, and his action in murdering his bride did him absolutely no good at all, for immediately after the deed was discovered, he was lynched by a furious mob in Alexandria.

All that was now left of the Ptolemaic dynasty was the illegitimate son of Lathyros, Ptolemy XII Neos Dionysos – often referred to as 'the bastard' or 'the flute-player'. He was married to Cleopatra V, his sister, and was the father of the last of the Ptolemys, the incomparable Cleopatra VII.

Rome had taken Cyprus, and Ptolemy XII's failure to act had not endeared him to the Egyptians. He was driven out of Alexandria in 58 BC, leaving his sister, Cleopatra V and their daughter, Berenice IV, to rule Egypt in his place. About a year later, Cleopatra V died and Berenice IV was now the sole ruler. She married Seleucus Kybiosaktes, but after a short marriage had him strangled.

The reign of Berenice ended in 55 BC, when her father, Ptolemy XII, retook the throne with help from the Romans, having Berenice executed; this was one of the prices Ptolemy had been obliged to pay in order to return to Egypt. He continued to rule until 51 BC, leaving the throne to Cleopatra VII on his death.

Cleopatra VII was just 18 when she ascended the throne in the spring of 51 BC. According to Egyptian law, however, she needed a consort, so she married her brother, Ptolemy XIII. She had become ruler of Egypt at probably the most dangerous time in the country's history. Cyprus, Syria and Cyrenaica had gone, there was famine at home, and dangerous enemies were at the gates.

Cleopatra was a strong-willed woman, however, and rather than lying low and hoping to escape the notice of more powerful nations, she dreamed of building her own empire. She made her presence felt in 48 BC, when the sons of the Roman governor of Syria were killed on her instructions, having come to ask for help against the Parthians. This not only alarmed the Romans, but also the Egyptians, who promptly had her overthrown, placing Ptolemy XIII as sole ruler on the Egyptian throne.

LEFT: Wall painting from the sanctuary of the temple of Ptolemy IV, Deir el-Medina.

OPPOSITE: Pompey's Pillar, Alexandria.

PAGES 416–417: Coptic basilica with Roman mammisi, or birth-houses, at Dendera, built by Augustus with later reliefs by Trajan and Hadrian.

OPPOSITE: One of the Roman mammisi at Dendera.

ABOVE: Kalabsha was one of the Nubian temples threatened by the rising waters of Lake Nasser. The temple was transported to its present position, thanks to UNESCO and German sponsorship in the 1960s.

PAGES 420–421: Lake Nasser.

Alexandria, accompanied by over 4,000 men. Despite riots, Caesar was determined to take control of the country. Cleopatra was not one to miss an opportunity, and had herself rolled up in a rug delivered to Caesar. Consequently, by the time Ptolemy XIII had his meeting with Caesar, Cleopatra and Caesar were already lovers, and he knew he had been betrayed.

Ptolemy XIII was captured, but his supporters launched a revolt, known as the Alexandrine War. Some 20,000 supporters surrounded Alexandria, during which time the Great Alexandrian Library and some warehouses were burned down. Caesar struck back and the troops were dispersed, but it is believed that Ptolemy XIII was drowned in the Nile. Caesar restored Cleopatra to the throne, on the condition she married her younger brother, Ptolemy XIV, who was only 11; this was despite the fact that Cleopatra was already pregnant with Caesar's child. In 47 BC Caesarion (Ptolemy XV Caesar) was born, and the following year, Caesar returned to Rome, bringing Cleopatra and the child with him.

But in 44 BC, following a conspiracy between Brutus and Cassius, Caesar was assassinated. Cleopatra fled and returned to Alexandria; neither she nor their son had been mentioned in Caesar's will. No sooner had she returned to Egypt than she had Ptolemy XIV assassinated, establishing Caesarion as her co-regent.

By now Egypt was in a pitiful state, having suffered poor harvests and plagues. In fact, grave problems existed throughout the Mediterranean, and Cleopatra was desperate that her son be recognized as her successor. She enlisted the help of Caesar's former lieutenant, Dolabella, and sent him the four legions that Caesar had left behind in Egypt. But the legions

For a time, Cleopatra stayed out of trouble, but Pompey, a member of the first Triumvirate (with Crassus and Julius Caesar), that controlled the Roman Empire, had been defeated at the Battle of Pharsalus. Pompey made for Alexandria, hoping that his guardian, Ptolemy XIII, would protect him, but when he stepped ashore Ptolemy ordered his immediate execution. Four days later, Julius Caesar arrived in

were captured and Dolabella committed suicide in the summer of 43 BC.

Cleopatra now decided to throw in her lot with the Second Triumvirate, comprising Mark Antony, Octavian (who would later become Augustus Caesar) and Lepidus, who defeated Brutus and Cassius, Caesar's murderers, at Philippi in 42 BC.

By the following year, Egypt was on the verge of economic collapse, but being interested in the Roman armies under Mark Antony's control, Cleopatra planned to seduce him. An opportunity arose when Mark Antony summoned her to Tarsus, ostensibly to reproach her for her lack of support during the civil wars, but ended up falling in love with her. The two then spent the winter of 41–40 BC in Alexandria, and Cleopatra knew she had him completely in her thrall. Antony, however, was already married. His first marriage had been to Fulvia, who had caused problems in Italy over the allotment of land to army veterans. Having incurred the wrath of Octavian, Fulvia was exiled in Greece and after staging a confrontation with her husband, fell ill and died. In an effort at reconciliation with Octavian, Mark Anthony married Octavian's sister, Octavia, who had been married before and had three children.

OPPOSITE, PAGES 425 & 426–427: Further views of the Kalabsha temple, Aswan.

Cleopatra, meanwhile, had given birth to Mark Antony's twins – a boy and a girl – while Octavia's first child with Mark Antony was a girl. Had Octavia produced a son, the tragedy that was about to unfold may never have happened.

Antony, meanwhile, was still involved in the long-running conflict against the Parthians. By this time, Octavia had produced another daughter, but she accompanied her husband on his Parthian campaign. Halfway there, he sent her home with instructions to keep the peace with her brother. Mark Antony arrived in Antioch and sent for Cleopatra. He officially recognized Cleopatra's children as his own and named them Alexander Helios and Cleopatra Selene. He then granted Cleopatra Cyprus, the coast of Cilicia, Phoenicia, Judea, Arabia and parts of Syria, which allowed Cleopatra to build a large fleet.

But he was defeated by the Parthians in 36 BC, by which time Cleopatra had produced their third child. Mark Antony returned to Syria in 35 BC, at the head of a ragtag force that had survived the disastrous campaign, while Octavia was in Athens, with troops and supplies and a strong desire to join her husband. Mark Antony sent her a message, telling her not to come as he was already with Cleopatra.

Octavian seized the opportunity to provoke Mark Antony, and war seemed inevitable; remarkably, however, Octavia remained loyal to her husband.

In the following year, Antony campaigned successfully in Armenia and after his return to Egypt, his children with Cleopatra were given royal titles. Ptolemy XV (Caesarion) was made co-ruler and named King of Kings, Alexander Helios was named Great King of the Seleucid empire, and Cleopatra Selene was

made Queen of Cyrenaica and Crete, while Antony's other son, Ptolemy Philadelphos, who was only two-years-old, became King of Syria and Asia Minor. Cleopatra stood above all as the Queen of Kings and dreamed of becoming Empress of the World.

Rome was forced to face the truth in around 31 BC, when Antony divorced Octavia, despite the fact that coins were already in circulation bearing her head. Octavian then declared war on Cleopatra, clearly fearing that Antony and Cleopatra would eventually crush all opposition and conquer the world, ruling the Mediterranean together from Alexandria.

Antony's navy was badly mauled at Actium in September 31 BC. Shortly afterwards, Octavian's armies landed in Egypt and Antony committed suicide in 30 BC. Meanwhile, Octavian had no intention of letting himself be beguiled by Cleopatra, and declared she would be publicly displayed as a slave. Rather than face humiliation, Cleopatra killed herself, by pressing an asp (Egyptian cobra) to her breast. This was a symbolic death, for as far as the Egyptians were concerned, for to be killed by a snake secured immortality. After Cleopatra's death, Ptolemy XV (Caesarion) was strangled and Cleopatra's other children by Antony were handed over to Octavia.

The death of Cleopatra brought an end to the rule of Egypt, for although Cleopatra had been a Macedonian by blood, she had ruled very much in the spirit of the ancient pharaohs. From now on, Rome would be the ruler of Egypt. Cleopatra had very nearly changed the fortunes of Egypt, and had luck been on her side, Egypt would have been the dominant force in the world rather than Rome. She had genuinely respected Caesar, having regarded him as her equal;

Antony had been another matter, having been seen by Cleopatra as simply a means to an end.

The Romans effectively took control of Egypt in 30 BC, and Rome remained a single, coherent empire until the beginning of the 4th century AD, when it succumbed to barbarian invasions and internal conflicts.

When Constantius died in 306, his son, Constantine I, became King of Rome; after defeating his rivals, including Licinius, Constantine became the sole ruler of the Roman Empire in 324. In 313 the Edict of Milan had declared the Roman Empire to be neutral with regard to religious worship, officially removing all obstacles to the practice of Christianity and other religions. Having already adopted Christianity himself, Constantine called for the First Council Of Nicaea in 325, which defined doctrine and brought unity to the church. He moved the capital of his empire to Byzantium in 330, renaming it Constantinople, and died in 337.

The Roman Empire was divided by Theodosius I in 395, becoming the Eastern Empire and the Byzantine Empire. After about 1100, the Byzantine Empire would start to decline and the loss of Constantinople to the Ottoman Turks in 1453 marked its eventual demise.

Meanwhile, Egypt continued to be ruled by Rome and Byzantium until the Arab conquest in the 7th century. Alexandria had long since relinquished its importance at the centre of the Mediterranean world on the ascendency of Constantine's Constantinople, even though Aristotelian and Platonic philosophy continued to be taught in Alexandria well into the 8th century.

Under the first Caliph of Islam, Abu Bakr al-Siddiq, the Prophet Mohammed's closest companion, Muslim armies vanquished Byzantium and advanced upon Egypt, taking Alexandria in 642. The Egyptians, however, were swift to adopt the new Islamic religion, and Egypt joined the expanding Arab empire, that would stretch from Spain to Central Asia. The Umayyad dynasty ruled Egypt from Damascus until the Abbassids took control of the Caliphate and shifted the political capital of Islam to Baghdad.

Ahmad ibn Tulun governed Egypt from 868, declaring Egypt an independent state and successfully repelling the Abbassid armies sent to usurp him. The rule of the Tuluni dynasty lasted for 37 years, ended by the Abbassids, who returned in 905, retaining direct control over Egypt until it was released from the Caliphate's control. Then came a period, beginning in 969 and lasting for 200 years, when the Fatimids held the balance of power in Egypt.

Ayubbid rulers took control of Egypt in 1174, the first being Salah al-Din Yusuf Ibn Ayyub, or Saladin, who retained control until 1192. Saladin had been vizier to the last Fatimid caliph, and when he died, Saladin assumed control. Saladin, a Kurd, also won notable victories against the Crusaders in the Holy Land. He was a romantic historical figure, who would eventually leave Egypt and occupy Damascus and other Syrian cities, though Egypt continued to be a base for his operations. The period of control by Saladin's successors ended with Queen Shajarat el-Dur in 1250.

The Bahari Mamelukes, a soldierly caste, dominated Egypt for the next 130 years, governing until they were succeeded by the Circassian or Burgi Mamelukes, who would control the area around Egypt for another 130 years until the arrival of the Ottoman Turks.

The Ottoman Empire took control of Egypt in 1517, though the Mamelukes would remain vassals of the Turks until Napoleon Bonaparte invaded Egypt in 1798. The main purpose of the French occupation, apart from Napoleon's wish to emulate Alexander the Great, was to create a canal through the Isthmus of Suez, connecting the Red and Mediterranean Seas. Such a proposal was unacceptable to the British, however, and in the Battle of the Nile, off Aboukir Bay, the French were defeated by a British fleet under Nelson. It was also Napoleon's ambition to capture the key port of Acre, but he received a terrible setback in 1799, when his siege artillery was captured by a British flotilla. After several assaults on the city, he and his troops gave up the attempt and made the gruelling march back to Egypt.

The country was returned to the Ottoman Turks, though the Mamelukes were to remain a force in Egypt. The British invaded in 1807, after the Turks had put down a major revolt, but were beaten back. Over the next few years Mohammed Ali, the Pasha of Egypt, killed as many Mamelukes as possible in an attempt to safeguard his own position.

By the time the Suez Canal opened in 1869, Mohammed Ali's grandson, Ismail, was ruling Egypt. But the country was now in debt and the British and the French, to whom Ismail and the country were mostly in debt, demanded that he abdicate. Meanwhile, Ismail's son, Tawfik, inherited Egypt, but another revolt in 1881 precipitated the arrival of British troops the following year. By September 1882 they had reached Cairo and the rebels surrendered to the British. Ismail died in exile in 1895.

While Tawfik remained a figurehead in Egypt, it was the British who actually controlled the country from Cairo. Lord Cromer was placed in control in 1883 and would rule Egypt for 23 years, superseded by Sir Eldon Gorst in 1907. By this stage, the infrastructure of Egypt had been considerably improved, and there were now trams, trains, department stores and shopping districts.

Egypt acted as a base for the British and Commonwealth troops in their campaigns against the Ottoman Turks during the First World War. After the war there were hopes that Egypt would be given its independence, but revolution was in the air and eight British soldiers were killed in March 1919, which brought about retaliatory executions. Egypt was officially recognized as a British protectorate the following month, dashing Egypt's hopes of autonomy.

The relationship between the British and the Egyptians struggled on during the 1920s and '30s. Egypt was not under serious threat during the early part of the Second World War, but by July 1942 the Germans, under Rommel, had almost reached Alexandria. Montgomery took control of the British troops in North Africa, moving them up to El-Alamein, where they dug in, waiting for reinforcements to arrive. Over the course of October and November 1942, Rommel and his Afrika Korps, along with his Italian allies, were shattered and sent careering back west along the North African coast.

But for Egypt, the scare was over, and it could now settle down to the question of independence. In 1952 there was a military coup in Egypt. King Faraouk I was deposed and an Egyptian republic was declared in June 1953. Gamal Nasser seized power in 1954 and nationalized the Suez Canal. The British and their allies failed in an attempt to seize back the canal in 1956 and from that point on Nasser was regarded as a national hero. The independence of Egypt was henceforth assured.

GLOSSARY

Akhet — The horizon, where the sun emerges and disappears.

Amenta — The Underworld or the place where the sun sets.

Amulet — A charm, usually representing a god, a sacred animal or a series of protective hieroglyphs.

Amun — The king of the gods and the creator of all things.

Ank — The aspect of a person that would join the gods in the Underworld. It was created after death by means of funerary texts and spells. It meant that death was not the end of a person's existence.

Ankh — The symbol of life, represented by a looped cross.

Anubis — The jackal-headed god.

Apis bull — A bull with specific features that was sacred to Osiris.

Atef crown — Worn by Osiris, it consisted of the white crown of Upper Egypt and the red feathers of Osiris's cult centre.

Aten — The worship of the solar disk, introduced by Akhenaten.

Atum — As Atum-Re, he was a god representing the sun.

Ba — An individual's personality

Barque — A type of boat in which Re or other gods sailed across the sky.

Bastet — The cat-headed goddess, the goddess of joy and music.

Birth house — A small temple attached to a main temple, its interior recording scenes from the divine marriage and the king's birth.

Book of the Dead — A collection of magic spells and formulae written on papyrus, which first appeared around 1600 BC. The text enabled the dead to overcome obstacles in the Afterlife.

Canopic jars — Used to store the preserved internal organs removed from a mummified body.

Cartouche — An oval or oblong shape, in which the pharaoh's name was usually written. It was designed to protect the king's name.

Coffin Texts — Spells written on the inside of coffins during the Middle Kingdom period. They were intended to help the dead to cope with the dangers of their journey to the Afterlife.

Demotic — A script developed in Lower Egypt during the 25th dynasty.

Deshret — The red crown worn of Lower Egypt, worn by a pharaoh.

Duat — The land of the dead.

Ennead — Taken from the Greek word for nine, this was a group of Heliopolitan deities, presided over by Atum. They were Shu, Tefnut, Geb, Nut, Osiris, Isis, Horus, Seth and Nephthys.

Funerary cones — Cones above a tomb entrance bearing the name and title of the dead person.

Funerary offerings — Either real food and drink or depictions of them.

Geb — A god otherwise called the Great Cackler. The sun was hatched from a goose's egg laid by Geb.

Hapi — The god of the Nile.

Hathor — The goddess of motherhood, love and happiness.

Hedjet — The white crown, symbolizing Upper Egypt.

Heket A goddess, often shown as a frog, and associated with fertility and birth.

Heqa A sceptre in the form of a crook, linked with royalty and the god Osiris.

Hieratic Abridged form of hieroglyphics, first used by Egyptian priests.

Hieroglyph Literally the Greek for sacred carving, used to describe the Egyptian picture language.

Horus The falcon-headed god. Pharaohs were considered to be human manifestations of Horus.

Hypostyle hall From the Greek meaning 'bearing pillars'. This was a grand, outermost hall of a temple, believed to represent a grove of trees.

Ibis A bird sacred to the god Thoth. Later on, the Ancient Egyptians believed the ibis to be the embodiment of Thoth.

Ibu The tent of purification where mummification took place.

Imhotep The architect, said by some to be the son of Ptah, who designed the funerary complex of the Pharaoh Djoser.

Isis The goddess of magic.

Ka A person's spirit or soul.

Khepresh A blue ceremonial crown, decorated with disks and worn by the pharaohs.

Khepri As a scarab or dung beetle, the god was symbolic of resurrection.

Khnum The ram-headed god, another creator.

Khonsu A moon god, son of Mut and Amun, and shown as a child or with the head of a hawk.

Khu An individual's spiritual entity.

Kush The name given to Sudan or Upper Nubia by the Egyptians.

Maat Both a goddess and the Egyptian concept of order, justice and truth, which the pharaohs were responsible for upholding.

Mastaba From the Arabic word for 'bench'. This was the style in which the Early Dynastic and Old Kingdom-period tombs were constructed.

Memphis A city in Lower Egypt, founded by Menes, and the capital of the Old Kingdom.

Menat A protective amulet.

Menhed A scribe's palette.

Mentu or Montu A war god, sometimes depicted with a hawk's head adorned with a sun disk and two plumes.

Mortuary cult Consisted of individuals who made offerings to nourish the dead.

Mummy Taken from the Persian word *moumiya*, meaning either a naturally- or artificially-preserved corpse.

Mut The divine mother goddess, queen of the gods.

Natron A naturally occurring salt, often containing sodium carbonate, sodium bicarbonate, sodium chloride and sodium sulphate. It was used as a preservative and drying agent during mummification.

Nebu The Egyptian word for gold.

Necropolis From the Greek meaning 'city of the dead'.

Neith The goddess of the hunt.

Nekhakha A flail made of leather, and associated with the god Osiris as a symbol of authority.

GLOSSARY

Nekhbet The protectress of Upper Egypt, portrayed as a vulture.

Nemes A striped head cloth, worn by pharaohs.

Nephthys The sister of Osiris, Isis and Set. Her name means 'lady of the house'.

Nilometer A staircase leading down into the Nile river, marked with a measure to record flood levels.

Nome An administrative province of Egypt.

Nu The watery abyss from which life originally sprang.

Nubia The territory from the first to the fourth cataract. Lower Nubia was situated between the first and second.

Nut A sky goddess, also a mother goddess with many children.

Obelisk A tapered pillar, often made from granite, and usually set in pairs at the entrance to temples or tombs.

Opening of A ceremony to restore the senses of a dead person, allowing them to eat, speak and breathe in the Afterlife.

Opet A religious festival that took place during the second and third month of the Nile flood.

Osiris The judge of the dead and the god of resurrection and eternal life.

Papyrus Used as writing paper in Ancient Egypt.

Pharaoh Derived from the Egyptian term 'per-a', which means 'great house'. It was used to describe an Egyptian king.

Pshent The crown of Upper and Lower Egypt, signifying a unified country.

Ptah A creator god, or the divine blacksmith or craftsman.

Pylon From the Greek meaning 'gate'. This is a monumental entrance to a temple.

Pyramid A funerary monument enclosing the tomb of a pharaoh.

Pyramid Texts Writings on the walls of pyramids during the fifth to eighth dynasties.

Re/Ra The sun god, often shown wearing the double crown of Upper and Lower Egypt.

Sarcophagus From the Greek meaning 'flesh-eater'. This was a stone container in which coffins and mummies were placed.

Scarab A dung beetle – a symbol of regeneration and renewal.

Sed A jubilee to celebrate 30 years of a pharaoh's rule. Another would be held every three years thereafter.

Selket A goddess depicted with a scorpion on her head and associated with the funerary cult.

Sekhmet The lion-headed goddess, and the destroyer of the enemies of Egypt.

Set Originally the god of wind and storms, but later the god of evil.

Shabti A figurine placed in an Egyptian tomb to act as a servant to the deceased.

Shen A loop of rope with no beginning or end, symbolizing eternity.

Shu A male god depicting dry air.

Sobek The crocodile-headed god, both admired and feared for his ferocity.

Sons of Horus Four gods depicted as mummies, one with a human head, the others with the heads of a baboon, jackal and a hawk. They were responsible for protecting the internal organs of the dead, contained in each of the four canopic jars.

Sphinx   A stone-cut figure, with the head of a man, hawk or ram on the body of a lion.

Stele   A stone or wooden slab, covered with paintings, texts or reliefs.

Tefnut   A goddess representing humidity. She was the twin sister of Shu.

Thoth   The ibis-headed god, inventor of the spoken and written word and the patron of scribes.

Vizier   An individual with executive power given to him by a pharaoh to deal with the administration of the country.

Wadj   A sceptre in the form of a papyrus stem.

Was   A sceptre representing male gods.

Weighing of the Heart   A ceremony after death, where the heart of the deceased is weighed against Maat's feather. If the heart balances against the feather, the individual is granted eternal life. If it

is heavier, it is given to the demon Ammit, the Devourer of Souls.

INDEX

ACKNOWLEDGEMENTS

Art Directors & Trip: Pages 60, 68, 73 right, 80 left, 89, 101 left, 103, 109, 119, 136, 138 left, 153 left, 157, 163 both, 166 right, 175, 186 left, 195 right, 197, 202, 222, 241, 251, 258, 263, 264, 299 left & centre, 302 both, 314, 333, 334 left, 335, 352, 353, 370, 400, 419. **Art Directors & Trip/Tibor Bognar:** Pages 86, 223 left, 239, 249, 250, 280, 355 right, 361, 367. **Art Directors & Trip/Roger Cracknell:** Pages 248, 415. **Art Directors & Trip/Jean-Dominique Dallet:** Page 101 right. **Art Directors & Trip/Juliet Highet:** Pages 40, 206, 207 left, 224, 226, 356, 357, 409. **Art Directors & Trip/Linda Jackson:** Page 245. **Art Directors & Trip/Mary Jelliffe:** Pages 43 left, 102, 189, 200 left. **Art Directors & Trip/Peter Marshall:** Page 331. **Art Directors & Trip/PL Mitchell:** Pages 14, 105, 132, 139, 209, 297. **Art Directors & Trip/David Morgan:** Pages 15, 20, 106, 137 left. **Art Directors & Trip/Patrick Nicholas:** Page 240. **Art Directors & Trip/John Pilkington:** Pages 135, 137 right. **Art Directors & Trip/Peter Robinson:** Page 210. **Art Directors & Trip/Helene Rogers:** Pages 6, 7, 8-9, 11, 12, 16, 17, 25, 26, 27, 28-29, 31, 33, 34, 38-39, 41 right, 42 both, 45, 46, 47, 48, 49, 54, 55, 56, 57, 58, 59, 62-63, 64, 67, 69, 70, 74, 79, 80 right, 82, 90, 92-93, 94, 98 right, 100, 104, 111, 112, 113, 116, 126, 127, 128, 129 right, 130, 133, 140-141, 142 both, 143, 144-145, 146-147, 150, 152, 154-155, 156, 158 both, 159, 161, 162, 164 both, 165, 166 left, 167 left, 168 both, 169, 170, 171, 172-173, 174, 176-177, 178, 181 both, 182-183, 184 right, 185, 187, 195 left, 200 right, 201, 203, 204-205, 207 right, 208, 212, 213 left, 214-215, 216, 217 both, 218, 219 both, 220-221, 223 right, 227, 236-237, 242, 243, 244, 246, 260-261, 262, 277, 269, 272, 273, 274, 275, 276, 278-279, 281, 283, 285, 286-287, 289, 290, 293, 294 both, 296, 300, 301, 303, 306, 307, 309 both, 310 left, 311, 312, 315, 316, 317 both, 318, 319, 320, 322, 321, 324-325, 326 all, 327 all, 328 both, 329, 330 both, 332 both, 334 right, 336, 337, 338 right, 339, 340, 344 left, 345, 346, 347 both, 348-349, 351, 354, 355 left, 362, 364, 365, 366, 369 both, 317, 373, 374-375, 376, 377, 378, 380-381, 383, 384, 389, 390, 392, 393, 396, 399, 401, 402-402, 405, 406, 408, 411, 412, 414, 425, 426-427, 430-431, 434-435. **Art Directors & Trip/Adina Tovy:** Pages 10, 65, 72, 77, 78, 83, 84, 191, 299 right, 410. **Art Directors & Trip/Bob Turner:** Pages 18-19, 24, 32, 35, 36, 37, 50, 51, 52, 53, 66, 76, 81, 87, 88, 95, 96, 97, 107, 108, 110, 114-115, 117, 120-121, 123, 125, 131, 148, 149, 151, 153 right, 160, 167 right, 180, 190, 192-193, 194, 196, 198-199, 229, 230-231, 232, 233, 234, 255, 256, 259, 265, 266, 268, 270-271, 277, 282, 284, 291, 292, 295, 304-305, 308, 310 right, 313, 341, 342, 343, 344 right, 358-359, 360, 368, 385, 386-387, 398, 416-417, 418, 420-421, 422, 438, 438. **Art Directors & Trip/Dave Saunders:** Pages 4, 61, 288, 298. **Art Directors & Trip/Jack Stanley:** Page 71. **Art Directors & Trip/Jane Sweeney:** Page 252. **Art Directors & Trip/Patrick Syder:** Page 188. **Art Directors & Trip/Joan Wakelin:** Pages 41 left, 43 right, 44, 73 left, 98 left, 122, 124, 129 left, 138 right, 194 left, 186 right, 211, 213 right, 338 left, 350, 388. **Art Directors & Trip/Roy Westlake:** Page 99. **Art Directors & Trip/Terry Why:** Pages 2, 247.